OneBook.

DAILY–WEEKLY

The Psalms · Part I

Brian D. Russell

Scripture quotations, unless otherwise indicated, are taken from THE HOLY BIBLE, NEW INTERNATIONAL VERSION®, NIV® Copyright © 1973, 1978, 1984, 2011 by Biblica, Inc.™ Used by permission. All rights reserved worldwide.

Scripture quotations marked ESV are from The Holy Bible, English Standard Version®, ESV®, copyright © 2001 by Crossway Bibles, a division of Good News Publishers. Used by permission. All rights reserved.

Printed in the United States of America

Paperback ISBN: 978-1-62824-320-8
Mobi ISBN: 978-1-62824-321-5
ePub ISBN: 978-1-62824-322-2
uPDF ISBN: 978-1-62824-323-9

Library of Congress Control Number: 2016907761

Cover design by Strange Last Name
Page design by PerfecType, Nashville, Tennessee

SEEDBED PUBLISHING
Franklin, Tennessee
Seedbed.com

CONTENTS

CONTENTS

Week Four
Creation and God's Revelation (Psalms 8 and 19) 41

Week Five
Security and Justice (Psalms 11–15) 53

Week Six
Security and the Messiah (Psalms 16–18) 66

CONTENTS

WELCOME TO THE ONEBOOK DAILY-WEEKLY

John Wesley, in a letter to one of his leaders, penned the following:

> O begin! Fix some part of every day for private exercises. You may acquire the taste which you have not: what is tedious at first, will afterwards be pleasant.
>
> Whether you like it or not, read and pray daily. It is for your life; there is no other way; else you will be a trifler all your days. . . . Do justice to your own soul; give it time and means to grow. Do not starve yourself any longer. Take up your cross and be a Christian altogether.

Rarely are our lives most shaped by our biggest ambitions and highest aspirations. Rather, our lives are most shaped, for better or for worse, by those small things we do every single day.

At Seedbed, our biggest ambition and highest aspiration is to resource the followers of Jesus to become lovers and doers of the Word of God every single day, to become people of One Book.

To that end, we have created the OneBook Daily-Weekly. First, it's important to understand what this is not: warm and fuzzy, sentimental devotions. If you engage the Daily-Weekly for any length of time, you will learn the Word of God. You will grow profoundly in your love for God, and you will become a passionate lover of people.

How does the Daily-Weekly work?

Daily. As the name implies, every day invites a short but substantive engagement with the Bible. Five days a week you will read a passage of Scripture followed by a short segment of teaching and closing with a question for reflection and self-examination. On the sixth day, you will review and reflect on the previous five days.

Weekly. Each week, on the seventh day, find a way to gather with at least one other person doing the study. Pursue the weekly guidance for gathering.

Share learning, insight, encouragement, and most important, how the Holy Spirit is working in your lives.

That's it. When the twelve weeks are done, we will be ready with twelve more. Four times a year we will release a new edition of the Daily-Weekly. Over time, those who pursue this course of learning will develop a rich library of Bible learning resources for the long haul. Following is the plan for how we will work our way through the Bible.

The Gospels: Twelve weeks of the year the Daily-Weekly will delve into one of the Gospels, either in a broad overview or through a deep dive into a more focused segment of the text.

The Epistles: Twelve weeks of the year the Daily-Weekly will explore one of the letters, sermons, or the Acts of the Apostles that make up the rest of the New Testament.

The Wisdom Writings: Twelve weeks of the year the Daily-Weekly will lead us into some part of the Psalms, Proverbs, or prophetic writings.

The Old Testament: Twelve weeks of the year the Daily-Weekly will engage with some portion of the Books of Moses (Genesis–Deuteronomy), the historical books, or other writings from the Old Testament.

If you are looking for a substantive study to learn Scripture through a steadfast method, look no further.

INTRODUCTION

We have now before us one of the choicest parts of the Old Testament, wherein there is so much of Christ and his gospel, as well as of God and his law, that it has been called the summary of both Testaments.
—John Wesley

The book of Psalms, or the Psalter, is a rich resource for God's people. In this book, we find prayers that serve a dual focus. The Psalms serve as God's word for us while at the same time modeling words for us to speak to God. Ponder that for a minute. God values our prayers so much that one entire book of Scripture serves as fuel for our prayer lives.

The Christian life involves following the risen Jesus as he leads God's people into the world to make disciples. As experience teaches, life has ups and downs. There are times of abundance and times of challenge. In all seasons, God invites the prayers of his people. The book of Psalms is an instructional guide to a moment-by-moment walk with God through the world.

The book of Psalms divides into five units, or books: 1–41, 42–72, 73–89, 90–106, and 107–150. This structure is embedded into the final composition of the Psalter. Just as the Torah of Moses (Genesis through Deuteronomy) consisted of five books, so, too, are the Songs of David made up of five books. This study will focus primarily on Book 1. The only exception to this will be the treatment of Psalms 146–150 in Week Two of this study. As we will see, Psalms 1–2 serve as an introduction to the Psalter as a whole by grounding the reader in two key truths. Psalm 1 emphasizes the need for a constant attentiveness to Scripture. Psalm 2 declares that we can have full confidence in the security of the future by trusting in God's reign. The book of Psalms reaches its climax in Psalms 146–150, which conclude the Psalter with five resounding psalms of praise to the Lord for who he is and what he has done. In between this introduction and conclusion, we will journey through the prayers of God's people.

The book of Psalms contains many types of prayers. The three core prayers may be stated simply: (1) Praise the Lord! (2) Help! and (3) Thank you! There are other types as well. Some psalms focus on God's kingship—sometimes these praise God as king and other times the psalm focuses on God's rule through his anointed human king or Messiah. Other psalms focus on the importance of God's Word, provide wisdom for living, or serve as affirmations of the psalmist's trust in God. Of these, readers are often surprised to learn that the most common prayer in the book of Psalms is a petition for help. Through these various types of prayers, the psalms give voice to joys, complexities, and challenges of the life of faith. This reality is what makes the book of Psalms timeless in its appeal. People of prayer can find words to express themselves to God in times when they are unsure of how to pray. John Calvin wrote, "I have been accustomed to call this book, I think not inappropriately, 'An Anatomy of all the Parts of the Soul'; for there is not an emotion of which any one can be conscious that is not here represented in a mirror." Athanasius wrote, "these words become like a mirror to the person singing them, so that he might perceive himself and the emotions of his soul, and thus affected, he might recite them."

We represent another generation of pray-ers looking for ways to speak to God. With humility and in anticipation of finding fresh astonishment and sustenance in these God-inspired prayers, let us begin our own journey into the Psalms.

If you are familiar at all with the book of Psalms, you've likely heard of the association of the Psalter with King David. David was a musician before he was king. The stories about David in the books of Samuel record him playing music for King Saul (see 1 Samuel 16:14–23) and singing songs at key points in the narrative (e.g., 2 Samuel 1:17–27). Just as Moses is associated with the five books of the Law (Genesis through Deuteronomy), David is linked with the five books of the Psalms.

About half of the psalms carry the title "of David." This phrase does not necessarily imply authorship in the original Hebrew. There are undoubtedly psalms in the book composed by David, but the various titles to the psalms (whether "of David," "of Moses," or "of Korah," among others) may also be dedications. Regardless, the constant refrain "of David" through the Psalter gives the book a Davidic feel and functions to serve key theological and interpretive functions. First, David modeled the life of prayer by showing that even a great leader must live out of dependence on God, not on human power. Second, the references to David serve to link the prayers and praise of the Psalter with real-life events. The implication is that the Psalms are prayers forged in actual life settings so that we can confidently use them in our daily lives. Third, since David was idealized as Israel's great king, the connections to David point to the hope of God's people for the renewal of God's reign and kingdom. As followers of Jesus, we recognize these longings are fulfilled in Jesus, and these model prayers continue to help us live confidently in the knowledge that Jesus will return triumphantly to usher in fully God's abundant future.

There are thirteen psalms that specifically link the content of the psalm to a context within the life of King David: Psalms 3, 7, 18, 34, 51, 52, 54, 56, 57, 59, 60, 63, and 142. For example, Psalm 3 invites us as readers to ponder David's state when he was fleeing from the rebellion led by his own son Absalom against his leadership (see 2 Samuel 15–17). This reference is meant to give a context for reading the psalm. We are to imagine ourselves in a desperate situation in which we are surrounded by foes, including people whom we have trusted deeply but who are now betraying us. The reference to David does not mean that we can only pray this psalm if we are in this precise situation. Instead, it shows how a righteous king such as David modeled prayer for God's people today.

As we pray the psalms, let us assume the posture of Israel's greatest king and lift our prayers to David's and our true king, the Lord.

WEEK ONE

Psalms 1–2

The Psalter's Introduction

INTRODUCTION

For our opening lesson, we begin at the beginning. Psalms 1 and 2 serve together as an introduction to all of the Psalms. These psalms lay a foundation for our journey through the Psalter. The compilers of the book of Psalms were intentional in placing Psalms 1 and 2 at the beginning.

A couple of observations make this clear. First, unlike the majority of Psalms, including 3–9, 11–32, and 34–41 in Book 1, neither Psalm 1 nor 2 has any type of title. Second, Psalm 1:1 begins with "Blessed [Happy] is . . ." and Psalm 2:11b concludes Psalm 2 with "Blessed [Happy] are . . ." These two psalms work together to provide an orienting framework for reading the book of Psalms.

Psalm 1 will ground us in the habit of continual and delightful reflection on Scripture as the means to living fully for God as individuals. Psalm 2 will ground us in the assurance that our future is secure in the Lord so that we can live confidently in the present.

ONE

Astonished by the Word

Psalm 1:1–2 *Blessed is the one who does not walk in step with the wicked or stand in the way that sinners take or sit in the company of mockers, ²but whose delight is in the law of the LORD, and who meditates on his law day and night.*

Key Observation. Scripture serves as our authoritative map for living as God's people in the world.

Understanding the Word. Psalm 1 proclaims an authoritative guide to *happiness*. It offers wisdom about how to make it through life *happy*. Our English translation uses the word "blessed" to begin the psalm. *Happy* is a better translation in 1:1 because Psalm 1 is talking about happy as a state of having been blessed. Of course, this is the result of God's actions. All of this begs the question: How do we live this way?

The psalmist recognized that the life of faith touches every moment and interaction. Look at the verbs in verse 1: walk, stand, sit. These are our options while we are awake. Psalm 1 has all of life in view. We must be mindful of how we live. We are God's witnesses to the world. We do not live apart from the world as God's missional people. This is not an option. Instead, we live in the world. The psalmist was not naive in thinking that we could avoid the world. The psalmist had a more audacious vision. The key is to be shaped by God so that we are *influencers* of the world rather than persons who are *influenced* by the world. This is the warning of verse 1.

Verse 2 offers the positive virtue and practice that serves as the guide and road map to the *good* and *happy* life. Its word is simple but not simplistic. It does not offer a short series of steps to happiness or a one-time seminar to receive a certification in the state of being blessed. Instead, it advocates an *attitude* and a *habit*. Verse 2 describes the happy person as one who *delights* in the law of the Lord and *meditates* on it moment by moment. These are the core practices that serve as the foundation for the book of Psalm's vision for life.

Notice that this is no mere rote or legalistic force-feeding of Scripture. It is a coming to Scripture with an attitude of *delight* that opens us up to the feast that is there. How do we learn to delight in the Word? Pray these words: *Astonish me anew with the riches of your Word, not so that I may become a master of Scripture but so that the Scripture masters me.*

Then ponder it deeply and continually. In the original Hebrew, *meditate* also has the connotation of speaking the text aloud. It is noisily enjoying the word like a lion growls over its prey (cf. Isaiah 31:4). Breathe it in. Breathe it out. It is your road map for the journey of your life.

Psalm 1:2 echoes God's word to Joshua in 1:7–8: "Be strong and very courageous. Be careful to obey all the law my servant Moses gave you; do not turn from it to the right or to the left, that you may be successful wherever you go. Keep this Book of the Law always on your lips; meditate on it day and night."

In other words, Psalm 1 as a presupposition and foundation to the journey of faith calls us to a courageous willingness to *read* and *ponder*.

1. What does it mean to be happy or blessed according to Psalm 1?

2. Who are the biggest influences in your life? Are they positive or negative?

3. What role does Scripture play in your daily habits?

TWO

Success in God's Will

Psalm 1:3–4 *That person is like a tree planted by streams of water, which yields its fruit in season and whose leaf does not wither—whatever they do prospers.*
⁴Not so the wicked! They are like chaff that the wind blows away.

Key Observation. Success is the faithful embrace of God's will in the present moment.

Understanding the Word. Psalm 1 does not merely advocate that the blessed person will constantly meditate on Scripture. The psalm itself models this by actually using the words of Scripture to make its point. We already showed that verse 2 echoes God's words to Joshua in Joshua 1.

Verse 3 draws from multiple texts as well. Virtually every word is drawn from another Old Testament text: Jeremiah 17:5–8; Ezekiel 47:12; and Genesis 39:3, 23. Like Jeremiah 17, the psalmist described the blessed person as one planted by streams of water. Like Ezekiel 47:12, there is always fruit and the leaves do not wither. Like Joseph in Genesis 39, there is always success. We'll say more about these in a moment, but the key is to recognize the need for the words of Scripture to permeate and shape us for our journey of faith. There will be good times as well as times of hardship. The Psalter itself, with its mix of lament, praise, and thanksgiving, demonstrates this. Scripture is our guide to navigating the waters of life successfully as the people God calls us to be.

Psalm 1 redefines success in terms of being near to God and achieving God's will. Success does not necessarily equate with material possessions or wealth. Success does not mean an absence of suffering for the righteous. When read in light of the texts from which it was constructed, the tree imagery of Psalm 1:3 becomes a potent call to choose the way of life. J. Clinton McCann aptly wrote, "The point of the simile is *not* that the righteous will not suffer, but rather that the righteous will always have in God a reliable resource to face and endure life's worst" ("'The Way of the Righteous' in the Psalms" in *Character and Scripture: Moral Formation, Community, and Biblical Interpretation*, ed. William P. Brown [Grand Rapids, MI: Eerdmans, 2002], 137).

God's people succeed because they are rooted in Scripture. The text from Ezekiel links the waters with the waters of life flowing from the temple. In other words, Scripture is a pipeline and conduit to God. The promise of success is *success* in accomplishing God's will. Verse 2 alludes to Joshua; verse 3 alludes to Joseph. God gave each success in different circumstances. Joshua succeeded explicitly in life; Joseph succeeded and prospered from the bottom up. Genesis 39 speaks of God prospering him as a slave in Potiphar's house and as a prisoner in Egypt. It is important for us to recognize this new matrix for success. It is living faithfully in the present moment to advance the will of God.

Verses 3 and 4 challenge us with a contrasting view of life. Will we be the successful tree or simply be blown about as chaff in the wind?

The key is our root system. How deep are your roots? If our roots are strong, we can be battered by storms. We can lose all of our leaves in winter. We can experience broken limbs. But at the end of the day, we will continue to grow and prosper as long as our roots are near the streams of life-giving water. This life-giving water is available to us today in the Scriptures.

As we seek to follow Jesus faithfully into the world today, will you find the courage to take up the Scriptures and allow their words to shape your life and guide you to true success in accomplishing God's work and mission in the world?

1. How do you define success?

2. How does Psalm 1:3 describe success?

3. What is the meaning of the contrast between the fruitful tree and chaff?

THREE

The Lord Watches Over Us

Psalm 1:5–6 *Therefore the wicked will not stand in the judgment, nor sinners in the assembly of the righteous.*

⁶For the LORD watches over the way of the righteous, but the way of the wicked leads to destruction.

Key Observation. Scripture teaches us to delight and trust in the Lord who knows and watches over us.

Understanding the Word. Evil and wickedness will not be the final word. God's way for the righteous will stand the test of time. This is not an arrogant posture that rejoices in the destruction of enemies. It is a word to us in the present to bolster our courage and confidence to walk in God's ways with Scripture as our guide. It recognizes that the way forward as God's people is not always easy. There will be desperate times ahead. In fact, beginning with Psalm 3, we find some of the most desperate prayers imaginable as God's people cry out to God for help as they seek to walk faithfully through the world as his witnesses.

Verse 6 ends with a key reminder of the agent of success and security. It is God. Scripture serves as our guide *only* because it grants us access to God. God is the one who secures our future and blesses our lives. The spiritual life is never a 2 + 2 = 4 proposition. It is dynamic and relational as we live and breathe and walk moment by moment with God. The way of the wicked ultimately ends because the way of wickedness and evil is purposeless and without meaning.

The Psalter will stress the need to trust God over anyone or anything else. There exists the constant temptation to trust in our own power and talents or in the security promised by a human leader or king. We must resist this temptation no matter how wonderful any human leader or institution appears to be (see Psalm 146:3–5). True security exists in the Lord alone, and Psalm 1 invites us into a dynamic relationship with God through the gift of the Scriptures. The voice of Scripture is our trustworthy guide through life.

The psalm's view of life is audacious even in its presentation. The first word of the psalm in Hebrew begins with *aleph*, the first letter in the Hebrew alphabet. The last word in verse six beings with *tav*, the last letter in the Hebrew alphabet. It would be like beginning a psalm with the letter A and ending with the letter Z. This is a poetic way of declaring the psalm's vision of two ways is all encompassing. Verse six reminds us that the Lord, who knows and watches over the faithful, guides our lives. In the Old Testament, the greatest demonstration of this truth was the exodus from Egypt. As followers of Jesus, we have now experienced God's climactic act of Jesus' life, death, and resurrection as the fullest expression of God's power to save and guarantee the future. Jesus is the living and breathing Word who calls us to follow him into the world on mission.

The Scriptures of the Old and New Testaments serve as our map for this life. Psalm 1 reminds us that the journey to true success begins word by word and phrase by phrase as we come to Scripture expecting delight and breathing in its life-giving message. This will give us the foundational roots to live as the people God created us to be.

1. How does Psalm 1:5–6 help us to understand the relationship between good and evil?

2. What is the ultimate grounding for our security and success in the world?

3. How does Psalm 1 encourage us to become students of Scripture?

FOUR

The Lord Secures Our Future

Psalm 2:1–9 *Why do the nations conspire and the peoples plot in vain? ²The kings of the earth rise up and the rulers band together against the LORD and against his anointed, saying, ³"Let us break their chains and throw off their shackles."*

⁴The One enthroned in heaven laughs; the Lord scoffs at them. ⁵He rebukes them in his anger and terrifies them in his wrath, saying, ⁶"I have installed my king on Zion, my holy mountain."

*⁷I will proclaim the L*ᴏʀᴅ*'s decree: He said to me, "You are my son; today I have become your father. ⁸Ask me, and I will make the nations your inheritance, the ends of the earth your possession. ⁹You will break them with a rod of iron; you will dash them to pieces like pottery."*

Key Observation. True security in the present is found in confidently trusting that the future is secure in God's kingdom.

Understanding the Word. Psalm 2 opens with the first question in the book of Psalms. "Why do the nations conspire and the peoples plot in vain?" If Psalm 1 offers clear instruction from a bird's-eye view on our individual lives as God's people, then Psalm 2 serves to offer a global perspective on the relationship between God's people and the kingdoms *and* the nations who do not yet worship God.

How can an individual live faithfully in an unholy world full of threats? By trusting in the Lord and in the Lord's Messiah who rules God's kingdom.

Psalm 2:1–3 reminds us of the dangers of living in our world. There are nations and peoples all around who neither know the Lord nor desire to practice faithfulness. In the psalmist's time, God's people were surrounded on all sides by hostile nations. During the times of the Bible, God's people faced domination from scores of nations: Philistines, Midianites, Syrians, Assyrians, Egyptians, Babylonians, Persians, Greeks, and Romans. Many Christians around our world today face *real* persecution that threatens their security and sometimes their lives. The conspiracies and plots of those yet to know the Lord can challenge faithfulness, but this psalm assures us that these plots will ultimately amount to nothing.

Psalm 2:4–9 offers the response of the Lord to the raging of the nations. We find security in our world not in our own strength or by trusting in political or military power. Verses 4–6 describe the Lord's response to the *real* threat of the nations as laughter! The nations surrounding Israel had superior weaponry and larger armies, but compared to the power of the Lord, they may as well have squirt guns and paper planes.

Yet God does not respond with overwhelming force or shock-and-awe displays of military might. His answer to the nations is to appoint a king who will serve as the earthly representative and leader of God's kingdom from Zion, that is Jerusalem.

Observe in verses 7–9 the language used to describe the king and blessings that the Lord pronounces. First, the Lord identifies the king as his Son. "Son of God" is not a biological statement. Rather it is a pronouncement of the king's position and role within God's kingdom. To be the Son of God means that the Israelite king was God's human agent through whom he would administer his kingdom. The word "today" refers to the psalm's original use as a psalm of coronation. Psalm 2 provides language for the occasion when God's people anoint a new king. Verses 8–9 offer bold statements about the Son's authority over the nations. The nations may rage and conspire, but the Lord is in control over all the earth and God's Son sits on the throne of God's kingdom to administer it.

Originally, Psalm 2 served to declare the power and prestige of the Davidic king who ruled from Jerusalem. With the coming of Jesus in the New Testament, Christians recognized that the words of Psalm 2 were ultimately pointing not to a mere earthly king but to Jesus. We will discuss this further in the following section.

1. What does Psalm 2 teach us about security?

2. What is the Lord's response to the chaos and insecurity in our world?

3. What was the unique role of Israel's king?

FIVE

Mission to the Nations

Psalm 2:10–12 *Therefore, you kings, be wise; be warned, you rulers of the earth. ¹¹Serve the LORD with fear and celebrate his rule with trembling. ¹²Kiss his son, or he will be angry and your way will lead to your destruction, for his wrath can flare up in a moment. Blessed are all who take refuge in him.*

Key Observation. The mission of God's people involves extending to all nations God's invitation of true happiness and security.

Understanding the Word. The New Testament writers quoted Psalm 2 more frequently than any other psalm because it provided language for understanding the mission and person of Jesus (e.g., Matthew 26:63; John 1:49; Acts 13:33; and Hebrews 5:5). As we read through the Psalms, we will encounter many psalms that have messianic undertones, i.e., they help us to understand Jesus.

The book of Psalms provides language for God's people to use in their prayers to God. In its original usage, Psalm 2 referred to a literal Israelite king. After the exile to Babylon (587 BC), Israel's monarchy ended. Yet, God's people continued to pray these psalms about kings as a means of asking God to restore his kingdom by raising up a new anointed king, or *messiah*.

Jesus fulfilled this hope. Jesus arrived and his first public message was the announcement of the kingdom (see Matthew 4:17; Mark 1:15; and Luke 4:16–21). As his followers, we echo his words every time that we pray the prayer that Jesus taught his first disciples, "your kingdom come, your will be done, on earth as it is in heaven" (Matt. 6:10). As God's missional people, our ultimate security is still found in the kingdom.

Psalm 2:1–9 grounds our prayers in the security of God's reign over all creation through King Jesus. Through his life, death, and resurrection, Jesus achieved God's victory and demonstrated that God's love and justice will prevail over all forces that attempt to thwart God's good and beautiful purposes for his world and his people.

Psalm 2:10–12 ends poignantly by issuing a call to the nations to submit to the Lord and his Messiah as a means of experiencing happiness. The end of Psalm 2 is critical for understanding the mission and purpose of God's people in the world. Psalm 2 is a prayer that grounds the future and security of God's people in the Lord and in the Lord's Messiah, but it is more than a prayer *against* the nations. It is an assurance of a good future. Moreover, it is a good future in which God invites all nations to participate. God's final word to the raging nations is *welcome* and *acceptance* rather than wrath. Of course the nations must turn from their own ways and serve the Lord. They must approach the Lord in *fear* and *trembling* rather than in the arrogance and antagonistic rage of verses 1–3.

It is important for us as God's people to remember his mission as we journey through life. The future is secure. No matter what we encounter in the world, we must recall that God desires even those who are against the values of God's kingdom to turn to him and find joy and happiness in relationship with him. Our mission is to embody God's character in/to/for nations in which we live.

1. How does Psalm 2 help us to understand Jesus and to pray "your kingdom come" with greater understanding?

2. What role do we play in God's mission today?

3. How would you live differently if you truly believed that your future was secure in the Lord?

WEEK ONE

GATHERING DISCUSSION OUTLINE

A. Open session in prayer.

B. View video for this week's reading.

C. What general impressions and thoughts do you have after considering the video and reading the daily writings on these Scriptures? What specifically did this week's psalms teach you about faith, life, and prayer?

D. Discuss selected questions from the daily readings.

    1. **KEY OBSERVATION (PSALM 1:1–2):** Scripture serves as our authoritative map for living as God's people in the world.

    DISCUSSION QUESTION: What role does Scripture serve in your life? How does Psalm 1 invite us to become students of God's Word?

    2. **KEY OBSERVATION (PSALM 1:3–4):** Success is the faithful embrace of God's will in the present moment.

    DISCUSSION QUESTION: What does it mean to be happy or blessed according to Psalm 1? How does Psalm 1 challenge us to rethink our understanding of success?

    3. **KEY OBSERVATION (PSALM 1:5–6):** Scripture teaches us to delight and trust in the Lord who knows and watches over us.

    DISCUSSION QUESTION: What is the ultimate grounding for our security and success in the world?

4. **KEY OBSERVATION (PSALM 2:1–9):** True security in the present is found in confidently trusting that the future is secure in God's kingdom.

   DISCUSSION QUESTION: What role does God's Son serve in God's kingdom? How does the Son secure the future of God's people?

5. **KEY OBSERVATION (PSALM 2:10–12):** The mission of God's people involves extending to all nations God's invitation of true happiness and security.

   DISCUSSION QUESTION: What role do we play in God's mission today? Reflect on how Psalms 1 and 2 offer complementary portraits of security and the blessed life.

E. Close session with prayer.

WEEK TWO

Psalms 146–150

The Climax of Praise

INTRODUCTION

This week we will jump ahead to the end of the Psalter. If the opening two psalms ground us for the journey ahead by introducing the key themes of Scripture and confidence in God's future, the final five psalms (146–150) serve as the climax of the journey of life.

If the Psalter is God's prayer book for his missional people, it is crucial for us to grasp the end of the story before moving through the Psalter as a whole. Psalm 1:1 begins with the focus on a singular person, "Blessed [Happy] is the man . . ." Psalm 150:6 ends the book of Psalms with a command to all creation: "Let everything that has breath praise the LORD." This final exhortation captures well the shape and focus of the final five psalms. The Psalter moves from instruction on how to make it successfully through the challenges of life toward a future that celebrates God's victory for all creation by inviting all creation to praise the Lord.

A quick review of how the Psalter unfolds is helpful as we continue our study. As we saw in Week One, Psalms 1–2 serve to ground God's people in the resources of Scripture as God's authoritative instruction and in God's rule over the nations through God's Messiah. These orient God's people for the journey ahead.

The journey through the Psalter is a difficult one. In the Psalms, we encounter the good and bad of life. There are celebrations of God's abundance and laments over the perceived absence of God. There are liturgies for giving thanks and historical retellings of the failings of God's people. There are praises for God's reign and confessions of sin.

The Psalter, however, does not end in ambiguity. The life of faith has a destination and the faithful will reach it: *the constant and perpetual praise of the Lord*. Through the journey, God has showed himself trustworthy and faithful. God has called his people to serve as ambassadors to the nations and the end of the Psalter demonstrates that this mission will succeed. If the introduction to the Psalter opened with an invitation to the nations: "Blessed are all who take refuge in him" (Ps. 2:12b), the Psalter concludes with an exhortation to worship: "Let everything that has breath praise the LORD" (150:6).

Beginning in Psalm 3, the readers of the Psalter encounter the most common type of prayer. This is the prayer for help. Scholars call these psalms of lament. Lament psalms teach us to pray in the midst of crises. The Psalter anticipates that God's people will experience trials and tribulations during their journey through life. Some of these will result from the ill intentions of enemies, others from illness, still others from personal or national sin, or from unnamed catastrophes. Laments dominate the landscape of Psalms 3–89. The message is clear. Hope for God's people is found *only* in the Lord. When the world does not make sense, God's people must turn to him in earnest and direct prayer. The message of the Psalms is that God will answer the prayers of his people.

Other types of prayers follow: praise hymns celebrating God's greatness, thanksgiving psalms that testify to God's deliverance from times of struggle, psalms celebrating God's Messiah, songs of trust, psalms of instruction, and hymns emphasizing the kingship of God.

This journey leads us to the climax of the Psalter: Psalms 146–150. These five psalms all begin and end with the exhortation: "Praise the LORD!" This serves as the final verdict on history and all eternity. The God who has worked to redeem all creation invites all people and even creation itself to praise God for who God is and what God has done and will continue to do. The final words on history will be love, peace, security, joy, justice, and mercy. This future is secure so God's people can worship extravagantly in the now and live holy lives in the present in anticipation of the coming full manifestation of God's kingdom.

ONE

The Lord Reigns

Psalm 146 ESV *Praise the LORD!*

Praise the LORD, O my soul! ^{2}*I will praise the LORD as long as I live; I will sing praises to my God while I have my being.* ^{3}*Put not your trust in princes, in a son of man, in whom there is no salvation.* ^{4}*When his breath departs, he returns to the earth; on that very day his plans perish.*

^{5}*Blessed is he whose help is the God of Jacob, whose hope is in the LORD his God,* ^{6}*who made heaven and earth, the sea, and all that is in them, who keeps faith forever;* ^{7}*who executes justice for the oppressed, who gives food to the hungry.*

The LORD sets the prisoners free; ^{8}*the LORD opens the eyes of the blind. The LORD lifts up those who are bowed down; the LORD loves the righteous.* ^{9}*The LORD watches over the sojourners; he upholds the widow and the fatherless, but the way of the wicked he brings to ruin.* ^{10}*The LORD will reign forever, your God, O Zion, to all generations.*

Praise the LORD!

Key Observation. Our true king is the Lord; there is no human leader who is worthy of our deepest trust.

Understanding the Word. Psalm 146 begins the Psalter's final flurry of praise with the psalmist who called himself to the act of praising the Lord. In verse 1, he twice repeated the exhortation, "Praise the LORD!" In the second phrase, he called upon his soul to join the praise. In other words, the psalmist invited the totality of all that he was to return praise to God. Verse 2 offers the response of the psalmist. He declared his intention to indeed praise the Lord all of his life. Notice that in verse 2, the psalmist personally identified the Lord as "my God." To praise God is to proclaim one's loyalty and relationship to the Lord.

Psalm 146 then turns to the main body of the psalm in verses 3–10. The focus is on trust. We praise the Lord because the Lord alone can be trusted to sustain and carry us through the journey of life.

Verses 3–4 set up a contrast between trusting human authorities versus trusting the Lord. There is a problem with human leaders. No matter how great they may be, their power is temporary and there is no ultimate deliverance or salvation in them.

One of the key questions in life is this: Whom do you trust with your life and loved ones? Psalm 146 knows that there is only one being worthy of this trust: the Lord. Verses 5–10 tell us why this is true.

First, verse 5 boldly declares the happiness or state of blessedness of each person who finds help and hope in the Lord. We saw the word translated "blessed" in Psalm 1:1 and 2:12. Now we encounter it here at the end of the Psalms. This is good news. Our journey through life has a happy ending.

Second, verses 6–10 give the specific reasons that demonstrate why trusting and hoping in the Lord is superior to trusting in human power. These verses celebrate God's actions and character. We can trust God because he is the Creator of all that exists (v. 6). The Creator and Savior of the world are one and the same. God is the true King.

We can trust God because of his eternal faithfulness. God is absolutely dependable to do the right thing at the right time every time. God has the track record to prove this. Verses 7–10 list tangible evidences of God's faithfulness. The Creator does not sleep on the job but continues to act for justice and wholeness for all including, in particular, those desperate for what only God can do—the oppressed, the hungry, the prisoner, the blind, the humbled, the foreigner, the fatherless, and the widow. In other words, God is radically for the marginalized. In fact, these states of need do not suggest that such persons *deserved* their condition, but instead the psalmist declared God "loves the righteous" (v. 8). The implication is that these very persons whom the powerful often overlook are part of God's people regardless of circumstances. The gospel is not simply good news for the powerful and connected; it is good news for everyone including the disenfranchised and disconnected.

Third, verse 9 announces that the Lord who sustains the righteous confounds the wicked. There will be people who choose to thwart God's mission and oppress God's people, but their day will come to an end.

Last, Psalm 146 reminds us that the Lord reigns forever. Therefore, God's people must praise and worship him.

1. What reasons does the psalmist give us for praising God?

2. Whom do you trust with your life and loved ones?

3. How does Psalm 146 teach us to pray?

TWO

The Good Future of God's People

Psalm 147 ESV *Praise the LORD!*

For it is good to sing praises to our God; for it is pleasant, and a song of praise is fitting. ²The LORD builds up Jerusalem; he gathers the outcasts of Israel. ³He heals the brokenhearted and binds up their wounds. ⁴He determines the number of the stars; he gives to all of them their names. ⁵Great is our LORD, and abundant in power; his understanding is beyond measure. ⁶The LORD lifts up the humble; he casts the wicked to the ground.

⁷Sing to the LORD with thanksgiving; make melody to our God on the lyre! ⁸He covers the heavens with clouds; he prepares rain for the earth; he makes grass grow on the hills. ⁹He gives to the beasts their food, and to the young ravens that cry. ¹⁰His delight is not in the strength of the horse, nor his pleasure in the legs of a man, ¹¹but the LORD takes pleasure in those who fear him, in those who hope in his steadfast love.

¹²Praise the LORD, O Jerusalem! Praise your God, O Zion! ¹³For he strengthens the bars of your gates; he blesses your children within you. ¹⁴He makes peace in your borders; he fills you with the finest of the wheat. ¹⁵He sends out his command to the earth; his word runs swiftly. ¹⁶He gives snow like wool; he scatters frost like ashes. ¹⁷He hurls down his crystals of ice like crumbs; who can stand before his cold? ¹⁸He sends out his word, and melts them; he makes his wind blow and the waters flow. ¹⁹He declares his word to Jacob, his statutes and rules to Israel. ²⁰He has not dealt thus with any other nation; they do not know his rules. Praise the LORD!

Key Observation. Praising the Lord opens us to the abundant future that the Lord offers to God's people.

Understanding the Word. Like Psalm 146, Psalm 147 is a hymn of praise to God. It begins and ends with the exhortation, "Praise the LORD." Psalm 146 focuses on God as king and his faithfulness in sustaining the righteous.

Psalm 147 continues in this vein and provides additional rationale for praising the Lord. Both psalms draw from the long history of God's people. Psalm 146 emphasizes the need to trust in God over human rulers. Israel's kings and leaders failed in their leadership. The sins of God's people led to exile, the ruin of Jerusalem, and the destruction of God's temple. The psalmist wrote from the perspective of deep loss and a longing for a new future.

At first glance, Psalm 147 seems to jump from topic to topic. The psalmist praised God for rebuilding Jerusalem and restoring God's people (vv. 2–3, 5–7, and 12–14), for his power over and in creation (vv. 4, 8–11, and 15–18), and for revealing his word and laws to his people (vv. 19–20). Yet when we ponder this prayer more deeply, there is a crucial message. Psalm 147 envisions the renewal of God's people. Yes, the past recorded loss and suffering, but there is a wonderful future in God.

The good news of this new future is that it all depends on the Lord. Israel's past is now past. Its future is open because God is willing, ready, and able to restore and renew the fortunes of his people. This is how the verses about God's powerful ability to create fit into the psalm. God's people can be fully confident in their future because the God who creates, who numbers the stars, whose power is vast and unlimited, who brings rain to the land, who raises up grass and vegetation, who cares for the animals, and who controls the weather with a word, is ready, willing, and able to act decisively to renew God's people.

How do God's people respond to this abundant future? With gratitude and praise. Psalm 147 offers a way forward through the chaos of the world—praise to the God who guarantees our future. This is a crucial word, especially when we are in times of want and lack. The answer is a deep trust not in our own abilities or in any human leader or institution, but in God.

Psalm 147 ends with a reminder of the key resource that Psalm 1 offers us for navigating successfully through the world. Unlike all of the nations, God's people have access to the Word of God. It is our guide as we seek to live faithfully for God's mission.

1. How does Psalm 147 teach us to pray?

2. What are the reasons that Psalm 147 calls us to praise the Lord?

3. How do the references to God as Creator serve to shape our praise?

THREE

The Praise of Creation

Psalm 148 ESV *Praise the* Lord.

Praise the Lord *from the heavens; praise him in the heights!* ²*Praise him, all his angels; praise him, all his hosts!*

³*Praise him, sun and moon, praise him, all you shining stars!* ⁴*Praise him, you highest heavens, and you waters above the heavens!*

⁵*Let them praise the name of the* Lord*! For he commanded and they were created.* ⁶*And he established them forever and ever; he gave a decree, and it shall not pass away.*

⁷*Praise the* Lord *from the earth, you great sea creatures and all deeps,* ⁸*fire and hail, snow and mist, stormy wind fulfilling his word!*

⁹*Mountains and all hills, fruit trees and all cedars!* ¹⁰*Beasts and all livestock, creeping things and flying birds!*

¹¹*Kings of the earth and all peoples, princes and all rulers of the earth!* ¹²*Young men and maidens together, old men and children!* ¹³*Let them praise the name of the* Lord*, for his name alone is exalted; his majesty is above earth and heaven.*

¹⁴*He has raised up a horn for his people, praise for all his saints, for the people of Israel who are near to him.*

Praise the Lord*!*

Key Observation. All creation owes its existence and praise to the Lord.

Understanding the Word. The thirteenth-century medieval monk St. Francis of Assisi penned a hymn beginning with these words, "All creatures of our God and King, lift up your voice and with us sing." Assisi was drawing on Psalm 148 for inspiration; his opening lines capture aptly the theme of the psalm.

Psalm 148 envisions a vast choir that includes singers from all parts of creation joining in the worship of the Lord. The exhortation, "Praise the Lord," again brackets the psalm and serves to link Psalm 148 with the other praise hymns of 146–150.

Psalm 148 breaks neatly into two parts: verses 1–6 and 7–14. In verses 1–6, the psalmist exhorts the heavens to praise the Lord; in verses 7–14, the psalmist speaks to the inhabitants of the earth. The assumption here is that the Lord stands outside each of these realms. As Creator, the Lord sits enthroned above the highest heavens and can look down upon all of his creation (Ps. 113:5–6). Psalm 148 imagines the heaven and earth praising the Lord. All parts of creation join together to worship and adore the Lord.

Verse 1 offers a general exhortation to praise the Lord from the heavens. Verses 2–6 present the specifics of those invited. The psalmist called out first to the angels and the inhabitants of heaven. They are to lift their voices to the King. Verses 3–4 then turn to the heavenly objects. Psalm 148 calls out to the sun, moon, stars, and rest of the universe to join in praise. This reminds us that no matter how vast and spectacular our universe is, it is part of God's creation and owes its existence to God. Moreover, all creation owes its praise to God alone. This is an implicit warning not to worship the creation no matter how beautiful and awe-inspiring it may be. Verses 5–6 emphasize God's power and sovereignty over all creation.

Verse 7 shifts the perspective by calling on the earth and seas to praise the Lord. Verses 7–13 exhort all of the various inhabitants of the sea and earth to worship God. This section calls all of God's creatures to join the chorus of the heavens. This includes the sounds of wild animals, the singing of birds, and even the music of the fish of the sea. Most of us have experienced the beautiful sights and sounds of the natural world. God declared his creation to be "very good" (Gen. 1:31). This psalm describes an all-creation celebration of the Lord.

Verses 11–12 focus on a call for humans to join in the heavenly and creational praise of the Lord. It is fitting that this psalm calls the kings and rulers of the earth to worship. This returns us to the theme of God's reign introduced first in Psalm 2 and echoed in Psalm 146. Verse 12 then includes all women and men of all ages. This psalm reminds us of Paul's words in Philippians 2:10–11: "every knee should bow, in heaven and on earth and under the earth, and every tongue acknowledge that Jesus Christ is Lord."

Our psalm ends with a reminder in verse 14 of the special relationship that the Lord enjoys with his people. God's people must worship, but they worship in the understanding of their role and place within God's mission. God's people serve as the hands, feet, and mouthpieces of the invisible Creator God who reigns over all that is. This role will be explored in detail in Psalm 149.

1. How does Psalm 148 depict worship?

2. What is the significance of the psalmist inviting all creation to praise the Lord?

3. How does this prayer challenge us to think differently about creation and our relationship with it?

FOUR
The Witness of God's People

Psalm 149 *Praise the LORD.*
Sing to the LORD a new song, his praise in the assembly of his faithful people.
²Let Israel rejoice in their Maker; let the people of Zion be glad in their King.
³Let them praise his name with dancing and make music to him with timbrel and harp. ⁴For the LORD takes delight in his people; he crowns the humble with victory. ⁵Let his faithful people rejoice in this honor and sing for joy on their beds.
⁶May the praise of God be in their mouths and a double-edged sword in their hands, ⁷to inflict vengeance on the nations and punishment on the peoples, ⁸to bind their kings with fetters, their nobles with shackles of iron, ⁹to carry out the sentence written against them—this is the glory of all his faithful people.
Praise the LORD.

Key Observation. God's people function as witnesses who testify to the nations of God's victory and greatness.

Understanding the Word. Psalm 149 moves the general call for all-creational praise in Psalm 148 to focus on the specific role played by God's people within the mission of God. Psalm 149 is a bold and daring psalm of praise that exhorts God's people to announce God's ultimate victory and live in light of it in the present.

Psalm 149 begins and ends with, "Praise the LORD." Psalm 149 provides the rationale for worship by focusing on God's victory and on God's people's role in proclaiming it to the nations. Verse 1 invites God's people to sing a "new song." This language is typical of the Old Testament worship of God for a new work of God's salvation (see Isaiah 42:10 and Psalms 96:1, 98:1, and 144:9).

The term "new" reminds God's people that his victories and acts are not merely past tense. There is an abundant future and God continues to move in the present to create it. Verse 2 links this new song to the worship of God as the Maker of God's people as well as their true King.

Verse 3 is critical for understanding the meaning of Psalm 149. It envisions God's people praising God with dancing and playing of timbrels and harps. The language here is important. A review of contexts where God's people deploy dancing and timbrels together in worship all involve God's people celebrating a military victory over enemies (see Exodus 15:20–21; Judges 11:34; and 1 Samuel 18:6–7; cf. Psalm 150:4). Significantly, in these contexts, the worshipers played no role in the actual battle. They either celebrated the return of the warriors from battle or praised God for his sole role in securing an abundant future for God's people. This is important because Psalm 149 contains imagery that may be misread as exhortations to violence. Verses 2–4 assume God's kingdom has been fully established by God alone without the aid of any human power or weaponry. As verse 4 reminds us, God "crowns the humble with victory" rather than calling God's people to fight literally against the nations to achieve victory.

God won the final victory through the life, death, and resurrection of Jesus. Jesus willingly surrendered his life to the violent and powerful as a way of pointing to God's future kingdom of love, peace, and justice.

What role, then, do God's people serve in God's mission? It is simple and audacious. God's people function as witnesses who testify to the nations of God's victory and greatness. They are to epitomize joy and gratitude to the Lord (verse 5).

Psalm 2 opens the Psalter by declaring the security of the future for God's people through the reign of God as represented by the Lord's Messiah. The nations were invited to find happiness and security along with God's people by aligning with God's purposes. Psalm 149:6–9 assumes God's victory over the nations. These verses contain violent imagery of battle but this language is metaphorical. God's people win battles not with weapons fashioned by human hands but by embodying faith, truth, and righteousness (see Ephesians 6:10–17). God's people testify to God's good future through praise and worship. This is the privilege and glory of all who align with the Lord (see Psalm 149:9).

This prayer of praise is a crucial reminder to God's people in whatever era we find ourselves of our mission to witness to God's good, great, and final victory. We do this not with displays of human power or the flashing of weaponry, but with our voices singing out the good news of God.

1. How does Psalm 149 teach us to pray?

2. What is the mission of God's people?

3. How does this psalm envision God's people responding to the nations that may rage against God and God's mission?

FIVE

The Chorus of All Creation

Psalm 150 *Praise the LORD.*
Praise God in his sanctuary; praise him in his mighty heavens. ²Praise him for his acts of power; praise him for his surpassing greatness. ³Praise him with the sounding of the trumpet, praise him with the harp and lyre, ⁴praise him with timbrel and dancing, praise him with the strings and pipe, ⁵praise him with the clash of cymbals, praise him with resounding cymbals.
⁶Let everything that has breath praise the LORD.
Praise the LORD.

Key Observation. The journey of faith reaches its climax when all creation sings praise to the Lord.

Understanding the Word. Psalm 150 brings the entire Psalter to a resounding and worshipful climax. Some variation of the phrase "praise the LORD" recurs thirteen times in this short hymn. God's missional people join together with all living beings to form a choir to praise the Lord! Psalm 150 provides God's people with the who, where, why, how, and by whom of praise.

Praise is directed to the Lord. Just as all of Psalms 146–150, Psalm 150 begins and ends with the exhortation, "Praise the LORD." The repetition is a reminder of the object of our praise and subject of our lives. The Lord is our

God and we live for his praise and adoration. It is vital for us as we seek to follow Jesus and serve in his mission to stay in the worship of the Lord.

Verse 1 calls for praise throughout creation. Praise is not limited to any sanctuary, whether it be the heavenly sanctuary or the temple in Jerusalem of old or even in our worship centers of today. Rather, praise is appropriate across the vast expanse of God's creation.

Verse 2 focuses on the why of praise. The psalm calls God's people to worship because of what God has done and who God is. "Acts of power" refer to the mighty deeds of salvation that the Lord has done. For God's Old Testament people, this included praising God for his work of creation, for the exodus from Egypt, for the giving of the Law, and for faithfully sustaining Israel. These acts of salvation testify to God's greatness. As followers of Jesus, we can add to God's mighty works the life, death, and resurrection of Jesus our Savior as well as for the outpouring of the Holy Spirit.

Verses 3–5 stand at the heart of Psalm 150 and give us the most comprehensive list of musical instruments in the Psalter. It provides the how, or means, of worship. The portrait of worship implied here is a praising of the Lord that is vigorous and loud. It is also one that deploys a full orchestra of sounds to add beauty, harmony, and symphonic texture to the voices of worshipers. This psalm calls for worshiping God for his victory. As we saw in Psalm 149, the use of "timbrel and dancing" (v. 4) often accompanied community celebrations of great military victories. Thus, worship in the present is done in anticipation of singing refrains of God's final victory.

Verse 6 brings Psalm 150 and the entire Psalter to a final climax by issuing an invitation. It is an audacious one. The psalmist calls all creatures to praise the Lord. This points to the goal of history. The end of mission is praise.

1. How does Psalm 150 serve as the climax for the entire book of Psalms?

2. What does this psalm teach us about worship?

3. How would you live your life differently if you knew that history ends in all creation praising the Lord for his victory?

WEEK TWO

GATHERING DISCUSSION OUTLINE

A. Open session in prayer.

B. View video for this week's reading.

C. What general impressions and thoughts do you have after considering the video and reading the daily writings on these Scriptures? What specifically did this week's psalms teach you about faith, life, and prayer?

D. Discuss selected questions from the daily readings.

1. **KEY OBSERVATION (PSALM 146):** Our true king is the Lord; there is no human leader who is worthy of our deepest trust.

   DISCUSSION QUESTION: Whom do you trust with your life and loved ones? What challenges do you face that make it difficult to fully trust Jesus?

2. **KEY OBSERVATION (PSALM 147):** Praising the Lord opens us to the abundant future that the Lord offers to God's people.

   DISCUSSION QUESTION: What are the reasons that Psalm 147 gives as the basis for calling us to praise the Lord?

3. **KEY OBSERVATION (PSALM 148):** All creation owes its existence and praise to the Lord.

   DISCUSSION QUESTION: How does Psalm 148 challenge us to think differently about creation and our relationship with it?

4. **KEY OBSERVATION (PSALM 149):** God's people function as witnesses who testify to the nations of God's victory and greatness.

   DISCUSSION QUESTION: How does Psalm 149 envision God's people responding to the nations that may rage against God and God's mission?

5. **KEY OBSERVATION (PSALM 150):** The journey of faith reaches its climax when all creation sings praise to the Lord.

   DISCUSSION QUESTION: How would you live your life differently if you knew that history ends in all creation praising the Lord for his victory?

E. Close session with prayer.

WEEK THREE

Psalms 3–7

Praying through the Darkness

INTRODUCTION

Psalms 1–2 serve to ground us for the journey of life. Psalms 146–150 articulate the future that awaits. Now it is time for us as God's missional people to begin the journey through the heart of the Psalms. The Psalms are God's prayer book for God's missional people. As God's people, God calls us to live and serve as his missional community that exists to reflect his character in/to/for the nations. Yet, as both Psalms 1 and 2 hinted, life comes with challenges. The world in which we live and breathe is broken and cries out for redemption. God's mission involves healing creation and reconciling humanity with itself and with creation. God's mission also involves inviting hurt and broken people back into relationship with their Creator who loves them.

When we follow Jesus into our broken world, we will experience joy but there will be hardships and challenges. God knows this and provides us prayers for all occasions, including those times when we are desperately in need of God's help. We call the psalms of help the lament psalms. As we noted in the introduction, there are more laments in the book of Psalms than any other type of prayer. This is good news. It means that God desires and invites us to bring even our greatest sorrows and most desperate pleas to him. Our God welcomes us in those times when we find ourselves neck-deep in trouble and recognize that we are helpless to save ourselves.

The laments may be the prayers of individuals or written as the communal prayers for groups. The laments cover a wide range of topics from prayers for deliverance from enemies, national catastrophes, illness, and even death.

The laments do not arise from a lack of faith. This is a myth about the prayer for help. Christians sometimes give the impression that we are supposed to be happy all of the time. We use phrases such as, "It's all good," and quote verses such as, "Rejoice in the LORD always" (Phil. 4:4), to give the false message that Christ's followers must always be upbeat and smiling. Sometimes even our worship services can reinforce this by only singing happy songs and offering positive and upbeat sermons. When this happens we paint a false portrait of suffering. Suffering is part of life in this world. People of much faith and little faith will all face challenges in this life. To deny this is to deny life itself.

The Psalter's inclusion of laments is thus a profound gift from God for those of deep faith who experience suffering as they seek to walk faithfully as God's missional people. When we cry out to God for help, we do this in the recognition of two realities. First, we recognize that God is loving, merciful, kind, and mighty to save. Second, we acknowledge that our current predicament stands in contrast to our understanding about God. Therefore, in our cry for help, we are asking God to be God and to save us so that we can live and testify to the world of his salvation.

Let's now enter the world of the lament.

ONE

Help Me, Lord

Psalm 3 *LORD, how many are my foes! How many rise up against me!* *²Many are saying of me, "God will not deliver him."*

³But you, LORD, are a shield around me, my glory, the One who lifts my head high. ⁴I call out to the LORD, and he answers me from his holy mountain.

⁵I lie down and sleep; I wake again, because the LORD sustains me. ⁶I will not fear though tens of thousands assail me on every side.

⁷Arise, LORD! Deliver me, my God! Strike all my enemies on the jaw; break the teeth of the wicked.

⁸From the LORD comes deliverance. May your blessing be on your people.

Key Observation. The Lord invites us to pray in the midst of overwhelming circumstances.

Understanding the Word. With Psalm 3, we move from the security of Psalms 1–2 to the world of lament. Psalm 2:12 reads, "Blessed are all who take refuge in him." The state of happiness promised in Psalm 1:1 and 2:12 is now long gone. Psalm 3 begins "Lord, how many are my foes! How many rise up against me!" The psalmist felt overwhelmed and surrounded by enemies. So what did the psalmist do? He prayed to the only Being who could help him—the Lord. This is the heart of lament. The God of Scripture invites us to come to him in our time of need. Our journey through the world will have times of triumph in which we can celebrate the victory of God, but sometimes we will find ourselves in need of a victory.

In Psalm 3, the psalmist faced the crushing challenge of foes on all sides. Moreover, the psalmist's enemies were taunting him about his own faith. In their view, there was no hope for the psalmist because God would not deliver. Reflect for a moment on a hopeless situation that you've experienced. Have you ever wondered if God would help you? There are always doubts during times of suffering. In Psalm 3, these doubts are compounded by the faith-quenching cynical words of enemies.

What is the best answer for a desperate situation and the taunts of opponents? The psalmist refused to take his future into his own hands. He cried out to God, but notice that he cried out not in unbelief but in deep faith. In verse 3, the psalmist affirmed his belief that God was a shield around him against his enemies. There is a future because God would lift up the psalmist. Verse 4 declares the psalmist's confidence that the God to whom he prays not only listens to his prayers, but will answer them. Enemies may surround the psalmist, but he has a key ally who reigns from "his holy mountain."

How then does this declaration of faith serve the psalmist? Verses 5–6 announce the psalmist's state. He was surrounded, and from human eyes, his situation may have appeared hopeless, but in the midst of chaos, he would sleep. What a statement this is! How often during a difficult time do we lose sleep and toss and turn in the endless torment of worry and doubt in the dark of night? Even more, the psalmist confessed a lack of fear regardless of the odds. He knew that there was a future because he *knew the Lord.*

Verses 7–8 record the specific content of the psalmist's prayer. He asked God to rise up and smash his foes in the mouth. This violent language may sound harsh but this is the beauty of the psalms. They are raw. The psalms are raw because life is raw. The psalmist relinquished violence by his own hands and trusted that God would do what was needed to save him. Why the prayer to break teeth? It is a request to reverse the circumstances of verse 2. Remember that the psalmist's enemies were *taunting* him with words. He is asking God to silence them. The prayer ends with a move from the individual cry to a vision for all of God's people. It is a confession of God's ability to save and the request for blessing not merely for himself but for all of God's people. This is a model prayer because even in the midst of suffering the psalmist never becomes self-centered.

1. What is the relationship between the psalmist's faith and his cry for help?

2. How does Psalm 3 teach us to pray when surrounded on all sides by overwhelming obstacles?

3. How does this psalm understand the rawness of life and the place of violence?

TWO

The Lord Is Dependable

Psalm 4 *Answer me when I call to you, my righteous God. Give me relief from my distress; have mercy on me and hear my prayer.*

²How long will you people turn my glory into shame? How long will you love delusions and seek false gods? ³Know that the LORD has set apart his faithful servant for himself; the LORD hears when I call to him.

⁴Tremble and do not sin; when you are on your beds, search your hearts and be silent. ⁵Offer the sacrifices of the righteous and trust in the LORD.

⁶Many, LORD, are asking, "Who will bring us prosperity?" Let the light of your face shine on us. ⁷Fill my heart with joy when their grain and new wine abound.

⁸In peace I will lie down and sleep, for you alone, LORD, make me dwell in safety.

Key Observation. Our cries for help assume that the Lord is dependable in his relationship with us.

Understand the Word. Psalm 4 is another individual lament or prayer to God for help. Psalm 4 divides into three sections: verses 1–3 describe the psalmist's situation and trust in God, verses 4–6 offer advice from the psalmist to those afflicting him, and verses 7–8 conclude the psalm with a statement of faith.

The psalmist's situation is more ambiguous than in Psalm 3. In Psalm 3, the psalmist faced the overwhelming experience of being surrounded by multitudes of enemies. In Psalm 4, the focus is more on the psalmist's faith and response to his enemies than on the actions of enemies or even on specific requests for action by God.

In verse 1, the psalmist began his prayer by crying out to God for an answer. The psalmist addressed God as "my righteous God." We often assume that *righteous* and *righteousness* are primarily legal/moral terms. In the Hebrew, these terms are *relational*. In other words, the psalmist was not praising God for his moral character. He was addressing God as *relationally dependable*. God acts "rightly" in relationships. Those in relationship with God can count on him at all times. This is the source of the psalmist's trust that is evident in verses 3 and 7–8.

Since God is *dependable*, the psalmist asked for God's grace and mercy in the form of answered prayer. The prayer implied in the psalm is not so much *against* the psalmist's enemies but *for* the psalmist and the rest of God's people that they prosper as they live faithfully for God in a world that does not yet know the Lord.

Verse 2 presents the problem, but unlike most laments the psalmist addressed the people causing his problem. The psalmist's opponents were dishonoring his good name, and they were following after what was false. This may be literally "false gods," or more broadly a way of life that stands in opposition to God's will. In verse 3, the psalmist affirmed his confidence of his relationship with God and of having God's ear.

Remarkably, instead of calling on God to thwart his opponents (cf. 3:7), the psalmist offered instructions for those who afflicted him (vv. 4–6). He responded with an invitation to live as God's people rather than following in false practices. The persecutors needed to end their plotting and actions against the righteous (v. 4) and, instead, submit to the true God by joining God's people in offering sacrifices and trusting in the Lord rather than in their own schemes. It is in the Lord alone that we can find true prosperity and security. There is no need to exploit others and act unjustly to make it through life.

The psalmist ended his prayer by affirming his trust in the Lord. God has provided joy in the psalmist's inner being. This sense of happy contentment is worth more than the abundance of his opponents' material riches. This joy leads to a true peace marked by a secure sense of well-being. Thus, the psalmist could enjoy the gift of sleep knowing that his life was secure in the Lord.

1. What made it possible for the psalmist to sleep securely in the midst of his troubles?

2. How does Psalm 4 teach us to respond to persecution?

3. Why is it difficult to trust God during difficult and challenging times? How does Psalm 4 offer help in facing such situations?

THREE

Recognizing Our Need

Psalm 5 ESV *Give ear to my words, O LORD; consider my groaning. ²Give attention to the sound of my cry, my King and my God, for to you do I pray. ³O LORD, in the morning you hear my voice; in the morning I prepare a sacrifice for you and watch.*

⁴For you are not a God who delights in wickedness; evil may not dwell with you. ⁵The boastful shall not stand before your eyes; you hate all evildoers. ⁶You destroy those who speak lies; the LORD abhors the bloodthirsty and deceitful man.

⁷But I, through the abundance of your steadfast love, will enter your house. I will bow down toward your holy temple in the fear of you. ⁸Lead me, O LORD, in your righteousness because of my enemies; make your way straight before me.

⁹For there is no truth in their mouth; their inmost self is destruction; their throat is an open grave; they flatter with their tongue. ¹⁰Make them bear their guilt, O God; let them fall by their own counsels; because of the abundance of their transgressions cast them out, for they have rebelled against you.

¹¹But let all who take refuge in you rejoice; let them ever sing for joy, and spread your protection over them, that those who love your name may exult in you. ^{12}*For you bless the righteous, O* L$_{ORD}$; *you cover him with favor as with a shield.*

Key Observation. Security comes through reverence—a humble recognition of God's greatness and our deep need for him.

Understanding the Word. In Psalm 5, the psalmist was desperate to worship the Lord in the temple, but his enemies blocked his path. These may be literal enemies or our own inner voices that tempt us to turn from God. This psalm invites us to ponder: *What kind of person do I need to become to pray this psalm with integrity?*

Verses 1–3 establish the lament. The psalmist called out to God for help. The new day had dawned and the psalmist began with prayer. He addressed the Lord as "my king" and "my God." These are statements of loyalty and relationship and imply a deep trust. The psalmist needed an answer from God.

Verses 4–6 detail the psalmist's plight. He desired to worship the Lord, but evil people were blocking the way. As we read the psalmist's words, his prayer invites us to reflect on negative attributes and attitudes that we may have in common with the psalmist's enemies. What are the types of persons who stand in contrast to the righteous? Persons who act wickedly, live arrogantly, do wrong, tell lies, and act in bloodthirsty or deceitful ways. God is not pleased with such persons. As we pray this psalm we must open ourselves up to God's work in our lives so that we may join the psalmist in his desire to worship God rightly.

Verse 7 contrasts with verses 4–6. Unlike the wicked, the psalmist could enter God's house because of God's faithful and loyal love. There is one key attitude that the psalmist embodies: *reverence.* This is a humble recognition of God's greatness and our deep need for him.

Psalm 5 ends with a long prayer for the Lord to take action on behalf of the psalmist (vv. 8–11) and a final declaration of the psalmist's faith (v. 12). The psalmist needed the help of the Lord so he pled for God's guidance and direction past all of his enemies. The psalmist did not know the precise way but he trusted that God, like a GPS, would direct his path so that the psalmist arrived safely to the house of worship (v. 8). Verses 8–9 are requests for direct action against the enemies. The mouths of the psalmist's foes were full of lies. In Romans 3:13, Paul quoted Psalm 5:9 as part of his description of human sinfulness. Our psalm reminds us of the devastating effects that human speech can have on others if used wrongly. The psalmist asked God to announce their guilt and banish them for their sins against God. The unstated assumption here is that the psalmist's foes were likely asking for the same to be done to the innocent psalmist. In verse 11, the psalmist asked God to act on behalf of all who take refuge in God and love his name. Notice the shift from individual concern to praying for all God's people. This is a key learning from the laments. Each of us has individual needs, but the life of faith calls us to remember our brothers and sisters too.

Verse 12 ends the psalm with a statement of confidence in the Lord. God is the protector, the one who blesses, and the shield of his people. With God's help, God's people can enter his presence in security.

1. What character traits does Psalm 5 assume that we, as God's people, live out daily?

2. Reflect on how Psalm 5 may help us in times when we find ourselves falsely accused.

3. How does Psalm 5 remind us of the relationship between prayers for ourselves and prayers for the community?

FOUR

Confessing Our Sins

Psalm 6 LORD, *do not rebuke me in your anger or discipline me in your wrath.*
²Have mercy on me, LORD, for I am faint; heal me, LORD, for my bones are in agony. ³My soul is in deep anguish. How long, LORD, how long?

⁴Turn, LORD, and deliver me; save me because of your unfailing love. ⁵Among the dead no one proclaims your name. Who praises you from the grave?

⁶I am worn out from my groaning.

All night long I flood my bed with weeping and drench my couch with tears. ⁷My eyes grow weak with sorrow; they fail because of all my foes.

⁸Away from me, all you who do evil, for the LORD has heard my weeping. ⁹The LORD has heard my cry for mercy; the LORD accepts my prayer. ¹⁰All my enemies will be overwhelmed with shame and anguish; they will turn back and suddenly be put to shame.

Key Observation. The Psalms model the necessity of confessing our sins and failings to the Lord.

Understanding the Word. Psalm 6 is another individual lament, but it is a new type of lament. Psalm 6 is the first of seven psalms that the church has traditionally understood as prayers for the forgiveness of sin. The others are Psalms 32, 38, 51, 102, 130, and 143. So far the laments of Psalms 3–5 have assumed the *innocence* of the psalmist. In Psalm 6, the source of the problem is the psalmist himself. In this psalm, he offered a model prayer to help us in those times that we have fallen short in our love for God or neighbor.

As we read this prayer, let us recognize the costly effects of sin and recognize that God hears our prayers. As followers of Jesus, we know the familiar words of 1 John 1:9, "If we confess our sins, he is faithful and just and will forgive us our sins and purify us from all unrighteousness." This is a promise of grace. But such promises are not a license to sin. Our sin is costly both to ourselves as individuals, to our communities, and to the world that God calls us to serve.

The psalmist began with the consequences of sin in view. He pled with God that the consequences be lightened by mercy. Verses 2–3 describe the psalmist's *internal* anguish over his actions. Whatever the psalmist expected to gain from his wrong actions did not prove worthwhile in light of the suffering that his actions brought. Verse 3 is poignant: "My soul is in deep anguish." We may understand "soul" as "my being." The psalmist was in torment and pled for grace, "How long, Lord, how long?"

Verses 4–7 give the specifics of the psalmist's prayer. In verse 4, the pray-er rooted his hope for grace in the Lord's "unfailing love." This is one of the core attributes of God and means "faithful love" or "love that won't let us go." It is the basis for the relationship that God has with his people.

The psalmist was desperate for God's grace because he had reached the end of what he could endure. His sin had produced bad fruit: fear of death, weariness from groaning, weeping rather than sleeping, and exhaustion. Furthermore, verse 7 suggests that he was also suffering at the hands of others.

It is not clear whether these are more enemies such as we've seen in Psalms 3–5 or if the foes here are members of God's people who are heaping guilt upon their fallen brother or sister. Regardless, the psalmist laid it all out before God.

The psalmist anticipated release from suffering and sin in verses 8–10. Scripture is clear: God forgives sin. This is true in the Old Testament and New Testament alike. It is good news for the psalmist. The psalmist looked forward to the scattering of his accusers. The psalmist also then testified to the grace and mercy of God. This is good for all creation. Once sin becomes past tense, the story of God's forgiveness becomes a powerful testimony to a world in need of recognizing that God invites all to come to him for healing and restoration.

1. How did the psalmist's sin affect him?

2. How does Psalm 6 teach us to pray when we have sinned?

3. In what areas of your life do you need God's healing and forgiveness today?

FIVE

Praying for Justice

Psalm 7 ESV *O LORD my God, in you do I take refuge; save me from all my pursuers and deliver me, ²lest like a lion they tear my soul apart, rending it in pieces, with none to deliver.*

³O LORD my God, if I have done this, if there is wrong in my hands, ⁴if I have repaid my friend with evil or plundered my enemy without cause, ⁵let the enemy pursue my soul and overtake it, and let him trample my life to the ground and lay my glory in the dust. Selah

⁶Arise, O LORD, in your anger; lift yourself up against the fury of my enemies; awake for me; you have appointed a judgment. ⁷Let the assembly of the peoples be gathered about you; over it return on high.

⁸The LORD judges the peoples; judge me, O LORD, according to my righteousness and according to the integrity that is in me.

⁹Oh, let the evil of the wicked come to an end, and may you establish the righteous—you who test the minds and hearts, O righteous God! ¹⁰My shield is with God, who saves the upright in heart. ¹¹*God is a righteous judge, and a God who feels indignation every day.*

¹²*If a man does not repent, God will whet his sword; he has bent and readied his bow; ¹³he has prepared for him his deadly weapons, making his arrows fiery shafts. ¹⁴Behold, the wicked man conceives evil and is pregnant with mischief and gives birth to lies. ¹⁵He makes a pit, digging it out, and falls into the hole that he has made. ¹⁶His mischief returns upon his own head, and on his own skull his violence descends.*

¹⁷*I will give to the* LORD *the thanks due to his righteousness, and I will sing praise to the name of the* LORD, *the Most High.*

Key Observation. The Psalms teach us to imagine and pray for a world of justice in the midst of injustice.

Understanding the Word. Psalm 7 will mark a transition in our journey through Book 1 of the Psalter. Like Psalms 3–6, it offers another lament for deliverance from enemies, but Psalm 7 broadens into a vision for global justice (vv. 9–16) and ends with a vow to offer thanksgiving and praise to the Lord (v. 17).

The psalmist opened with a clear statement of trust as well as a plea for help (vv. 1–2). Trouble was near (again!) so there was only one response for the psalmist: turn immediately to the only One who can protect and save— the Lord. The psalmist asked for deliverance from ravaging enemies whom he likened to a pride of lions. He grounded his request in recognizing the Lord as his refuge but also adamantly proclaimed his personal innocence. In verses 3–5, the psalmist was bold in his prayer. God should respond immediately with deliverance because of the psalmist's *innocence*. In fact, the psalmist asked God to allow his enemies to kill him (v. 5) if he was in fact guilty of *any* injustice. Wow. Reflect on this for a few moments: *What kind of person do I need to become to pray Psalm 7 with such confidence?*

In verses 6–8, the psalmist made direct requests for salvation. The assumption was that he was indeed *innocent*. Therefore, God should act and must act. This is prayer at its best. Prayer assumes a dynamic relationship between God and the one praying. We can present ourselves openly and honestly to God and hold nothing back in the assumption that God will hear us and respond.

Remarkably, given the predicament of the psalmist, the psalmist expanded the scope of the prayer to include all who were innocent (vv. 9–16). He imagined a world marked by the rule of justice and the end of injustice. He begged God to act *against* those who practiced evil and injustice against those who sought to live rightly in love for God and neighbor.

The psalmist trusted that God is a warrior who will protect the innocent from those with ill intentions. Notice that he relinquished all vengeance to God rather than taking action himself. The psalmist expected and awaited God's righteous actions to establish justice.

Verse 17 ends the psalm with a vow of thanksgiving and praise of the Lord who reigns from on high. This vow will be fulfilled in Psalm 8, which begins, "Lord, our Lord, how majestic is your name in all the earth!" Thanksgiving and praise is fitting for the Lord who is righteous and acts on behalf of his children. Gratitude is a critical response to God's graciousness and keeps us mindful of God's ongoing work in our lives.

1. How does Psalm 7 teach to expand our prayers beyond our own needs?

2. How does the psalmist's view of God's righteous actions encourage us in our times of need?

3. What role does thanksgiving and praise play in your life of faith?

WEEK THREE

GATHERING DISCUSSION OUTLINE

A. Open session in prayer.

B. View video for this week's reading.

C. What general impressions and thoughts do you have after considering the video and reading the daily writings on these Scriptures? What specifically did this week's psalms teach you about faith, life, and prayer?

D. Discuss selected questions from the daily readings.

    1. **KEY OBSERVATION (PSALM 3):** The Lord invites us to pray in the midst of overwhelming circumstances.

        DISCUSSION QUESTION: How does this psalm teach us to pray when surrounded on all sides by overwhelming obstacles?

    2. **KEY OBSERVATION (PSALM 4):** Our cries for help assume that the Lord is dependable in his relationship with us.

        DISCUSSION QUESTION: Why is it difficult to trust God during difficult and challenging times? What does the psalmist teach us about faith?

    3. **KEY OBSERVATION (PSALM 5):** Security comes through reverence—a humble recognition of God's greatness and our deep need for him.

        DISCUSSION QUESTION: Reflect on how Psalm 5 may help us in times when we find ourselves falsely accused.

4. **KEY OBSERVATION (PSALM 6):** The Psalms model the necessity of confessing our sins and failings to the Lord.

   DISCUSSION QUESTION: How has the psalmist's sin affected him? How does Psalm 6 teach us to pray when we have sinned?

5. **KEY OBSERVATION (PSALM 7):** The Psalms teach us to imagine and pray for a world of justice in the midst of injustice.

   DISCUSSION QUESTION: How does the psalmist's view of God's righteous actions encourage us in our times of need?

E. Close session with prayer.

WEEK FOUR

Psalms 8 and 19

Creation and God's Revelation

INTRODUCTION

In this week's lesson, we turn to two psalms of praise: Psalm 8 and Psalm 19. Psalm 8 immediately fulfills the vow to praise God found in Psalm 7:17. Psalm 19 is a slightly different type of praise psalm; it is a psalm that lifts up the power and necessity of God's Torah, or law for the life of faith.

Both psalms ground the praise of God in creation. Scripture affirms that God is both Creator and Savior. Psalms 8 and 19 unite these themes.

Psalm 8 is the first praise hymn in the Psalter. It begins and ends with the exhortation: "LORD, our Lord, how majestic is your name in all the earth!" (vv. 1 and 9). Psalm 8 is full of a deep hope in the Lord. It offers a powerful counter-testimony to the chaos of the world that gives rise to our laments. Human power and privilege are not the final words. The Lord is present in and over all creation. His power and majesty guide and govern history. God does not have to rely on the rants of the cruel or violent. God can establish his victory through praise of children (v. 2). Psalm 8 revels in the wonder of creation and in the special role that God designed for men and women.

Psalm 19 is a beautifully crafted prayer. C. S. Lewis wrote in *Reflections on the Psalms*, "I take this to be the greatest poem in the Psalter and one of the greatest lyrics in the world." It can be broken into three sections: verses 1–6; 7–10; and 11–14. Verses 1–6 recount the witness of the heavens. Verses 7–10 describe the potency of the revelation of God in the Law. Finally, verses 11–14 describe the response of the psalmist to the preceding verses.

Psalm 19 includes elements of praise and petition. It opens with a sense of awe at the distinct witness of creation to its Creator (vv. 1–6). The praise continues but shifts to focus on the power of the Lord's concrete revelation to his people in the form of the Torah (vv. 7–10). The psalm concludes with the psalmist recognizing his or her own need before the shining light of God's Word (vv. 11–14). In verse 14, the psalm comes full circle with a request by the psalmist for cleansing so that he may join in the praise of the Lord in concert with the voices of the heavens.

Psalm 19 thus reminds God's people of the need for ongoing transformation as they seek to witness to the world about the identity and mighty acts of the Lord.

Both Psalm 8 and 19 will also help us to understand how Jesus' life and ministry served to bring the prayers and praises of these psalms to their greatest fulfillment.

ONE

The Greatness of the Lord

Psalm 8:1–2 LORD, *our Lord, how majestic is your name in all the earth!*
You have set your glory in the heavens. [2]*Through the praise of children and infants you have established a stronghold against your enemies, to silence the foe and the avenger.*

Key Observation. Praise reminds God's people of the greatness and majesty of the Lord.

Understanding the Word. In Psalm 8, we encounter the first hymn of praise in the Psalter. Its opening and closing lines (vv. 1 and 9) exhort us to sing of the majesty of the name the Lord. This psalm then focuses its praise for God as Creator of all but especially for the role that the Lord graciously created men and women to fill.

The opening and closing exhortations praise God for the majesty and wonder of God's name "LORD" *in all the earth.* This psalm reminds us that the God of the Bible is not restricted to any small slice of the world. His name is not confined in a temple, room, tree, rock, or in any particular part of the created world. The entire earth is the sphere of his awesomeness. The words of the seraphim in Isaiah 6:3 carry similar meaning: "Holy, holy, holy is the LORD Almighty; the whole earth is full of his glory."

Verses 1–2 connect the heavens and the earth in terms of the proclamation of God's glory or splendor. There was no doubt in the psalmist's mind of the Lord's *worthiness* to be worshiped. Verse 2 is difficult in its specific meaning but its general meaning is clear. English translations differ. Our NIV text uses the word "praise." The Hebrew literally reads, "Out of the mouths of children and infants you've established strength." The idea is that God has created a world where human *power* is not the final word in history. The sounds of the weak, whether they are the praise of God or not, can silence powerful enemies. God has created a world that privileges light, justice, peace, love, grace, and mercy. These are the values of God's kingdom.

In our lives on the earth, we often face the hostility of forces that privilege power, darkness, injustice, war, envy, division, vengeance, and hate. These forces often seem more powerful than God and at times seem poised and ready to sweep us away. Psalms 3–7 remind us of the challenges of living the journey of faith. There are perils that drive us to cry out for help.

Psalm 8 speaks a counter-testimony against the powers of darkness for the way of God. God establishes a different mode of living. It is one that finds power in the margins rather than in places of privilege. Within the awesomeness of creation, God is sovereign and powerful. To demonstrate divine power, God's kingdom advances through different channels than does the world's power. In the world, whoever speaks the loudest and most forcefully often carries the day. Psalm 8 declares that strength manifests through the voices of children. This truth astonished the psalmist. God empowers the weak to serve as mouthpieces of God's power. This stands as testimony to the world and invites all creation to rejoice in God's majesty.

1. How does Psalm 8 describe the praise of God?

2. How does Psalm 8 help us to understand God's work in the world?

3. How does the psalmist's understanding of weakness challenge our culture's focus on the wealthy, the talented, and the beautiful?

TWO

Humanity as Creation's Climax

Psalm 8:3–9 *When I consider your heavens, the work of your fingers, the moon and the stars, which you have set in place, ⁴what is mankind that you are mindful of them, human beings that you care for them?*

⁵You have made them a little lower than the angels and crowned them with glory and honor. ⁶You made them rulers over the works of your hands; you put everything under their feet: ⁷all flocks and herds, and the animals of the wild, ⁸the birds in the sky, and the fish in the sea, all that swim the paths of the seas.

⁹LORD, our Lord, how majestic is your name in all the earth!

Key Observation. God created humanity as the climax of creation; Jesus models this way of life for us.

Understanding the Word. The psalmist stood in awe when contemplating God's marvelous creation on one hand and on the other hand humanity's place within it. God shaped the universe in all its vastness yet God invites humanity into a special relationship. Verse 4 asks this question in a way that captures the psalmist's wonder: "What is mankind that you are mindful of them, human beings that you care for them?"

Verses 5–8 reflect on the place of women and men in God's world. Much of the language here comes from the creation account of humanity in Genesis 1:26–31. Scripture announces that God has crafted every single person who has ever lived and ever will in God's image. This lifts up the dignity of *every* person regardless of economic status, gender, ethnicity, or any other idea or belief that divides our world. This was a unique idea in the ancient world of the psalmist. In the ancient world, only kings were thought to be in God's image and this gave them a license to use and abuse other humans as expendable slaves and servants of the king and the gods. The biblical view of humanity is sharply different. The Bible views every person as *kings* and *queens*. All of us have value. This is the truth that the psalmist marveled about.

God created people to serve in God's mission as stewards over all creation and as witnesses of God's character to the rest of creation. In light of this good news, the psalmist returned to his initial exhortation: "O LORD our Lord, how majestic is your name in all the earth!" (v. 9).

We may object and ask, "Where do we see this truth manifest in our day?" In Scripture, the reality described by Psalm 8 finds its fullest manifestation in Jesus' life, death, and resurrection.

In Hebrews 2:6–11, the author connected the hope expressed in Psalm 8:4–6 with the work of Jesus. Jesus came to fulfill God's original intentions for all humanity. Jesus lived the perfect human life in anticipation of the full renewal of all things through his death and resurrection. Through Jesus' faithful life and sacrificial death, he offered the opportunity for all people to receive God's grace, be made holy, and be reconciled fully to God's family (see Hebrews 2:11). Jesus came to make it possible for each of us to live as the person God created us to be. This is good news. Psalm 8 marvels at the possibilities and potentials of each person. It envisions a different type of world.

With the coming of Jesus and his death and resurrection, we as Jesus' followers can begin to witness through our own lives and serve in God's mission to manifest God's future abundance in the now while we await its full manifestation in the coming New Creation.

1. What does Psalm 8 remind us about the role of humanity in God's creation?

2. What does this psalm teach us about Jesus' life and mission?

3. How does this psalm help us to understand our mission?

THREE

Heaven's Declaration

Psalm 19:1–6 *The heavens declare the glory of God; the skies proclaim the work of his hands. ²Day after day they pour forth speech; night after night they reveal knowledge. ³They have no speech, they use no words; no sound is heard from them. ⁴Yet their voice goes out into all the earth, their words to the ends of the world. In the heavens God has pitched a tent for the sun. ⁵It is like a bridegroom coming out of his chamber, like a champion rejoicing to run his course. ⁶It rises* *at one end of the heavens and makes its circuit to the other; nothing is deprived of its warmth.*

Key Observation. Creation points to the Creator.

Understanding the Word. Psalm 19 reorients us to the Torah as a source of strength and sustenance for the journey. Psalm 18 witnesses to the guidance of the Lord's teaching (v. 22). Psalm 19 bears a deeper testimony to it.

Psalm 19 includes elements of praise and petition. It opens with a sense of awe at the distinct witness of creation to its Creator (vv. 1–6). The praise continues but shifts to focus on the power of the Lord's concrete revelation to God's people in the form of the Torah (vv. 7–10). The psalm concludes with the psalmist recognizing his or her own need before the shining light of God's Word (vv. 11–14). In verse 14, the psalm comes full circle with a request by the psalmist for cleansing so that he may join in the praise of the Lord in concert with the voices of the heavens.

Psalm 19 begins by reflecting on the witness to God by the creation itself. As we saw in our review of Psalms 146–150, the final psalms (especially 148 and 150) anticipate an all-creation praise of the Lord. Psalm 19 opens memorably, "The heavens declare the glory of God." *Glory* refers to God's awesomeness or weightiness. There is a witness in creation about the Creator. It is interesting that in Psalm 19 two different words for God are deployed. In verse 1, it is a generic word "God" that could be used of any god. Obviously, the psalmist had Israel's God in mind, but it is notable that God's personal name "Lord" is found only from verses 7–14 when the witness of the Torah is in view.

Why is this? This is part of the beauty of Psalm 19. Creation offers a witness to the reality of the divine, but look at verses 2–4. There is revelation about God but it is not clear or specific. When we ponder the beauty and grandeur of creation, we can recognize the hand of the Creator, but we do not gain specific knowledge of God's character, mission, or will.

Of creation's witness, Paul wrote these words in Romans 1:20, "For since the creation of the world God's invisible qualities—his eternal power and divine nature—have been clearly seen, being understood from what has been made, so that people are without excuse." Thus, nature shows us that there is a Creator. But we, as persons seeking to know God, need more.

We desire to know: Who is God? What is God's will? We need a clear word from God.

Psalm 19 transitions to the next section by reflecting on the sun in verses 4–6. The sun is everywhere and brings its life-giving warmth to the entire earth. As we will see, the Law, or Torah, of the Lord will serve in this role for people. It will be the Law of the Lord that provides clear instruction and transformative truth to guide us through the world.

1. How does nature proclaim God's glory?

2. What is your personal experience of nature's message about God?

3. What are the limitations of nature's revelation?

FOUR

The Revelation from Scripture

Psalm 19:7–10 *The law of the LORD is perfect, refreshing the soul. The statutes of the LORD are trustworthy, making wise the simple. ⁸The precepts of the LORD are right, giving joy to the heart. The commands of the LORD are radiant, giving light to the eyes. ⁹The fear of the LORD is pure, enduring forever. The decrees of the LORD are firm, and all of them are righteous.*

¹⁰They are more precious than gold, than much pure gold; they are sweeter than honey, than honey from the honeycomb.

Key Observation. Scripture reveals the truth of creation and our need for God.

Understanding the Word. Psalm 19:7–10 marks a return to the theme of the first psalm: the *power* of Scripture and the *essential* role that it serves the people of God. Psalm 19 is the second of three psalms in the Psalter that focus on Scripture: Psalms 1, 19, and 119. Scholars refer to these three psalms as Torah psalms. *Torah* refers to the authoritative instruction that God delivered to Moses at Sinai for God's people. These psalms serve to orient God's people to their core Scripture. According to Psalm 1, God's people can experience a true happy state of existence by allowing God's Word to permeate and shape their lives. Psalm 19:7–10 re-roots God's people in the Torah after the heavy dose of lament psalms that precede it. Psalm 19 reflects on the power of the Torah to transform people.

Scripture is an essential part of the journey of God's people through the world as they seek to live as his missional community that reflects his character. As we learn to pray as we follow Jesus into the world on mission, we've already felt the power of the laments and experienced the unbridled sense of wonder in Israel's praise (both within the lament psalms as well as in the hymn of Psalm 8). Psalm 19:7–10 reorients us to the Torah as a source of transforming truth as we seek to live faithfully as God's missional people.

In verses 7–9, we find six lines which follow a recurring pattern: (1) six synonyms for Torah: law, statutes, precepts, commands, fear, and decrees; (2) six recurrences of Lord; (3) six adjectives that provide an attribute of Torah: perfect, trustworthy, right, radiant, pure, and firm; and (4) six results or effects of Torah: refreshing the soul, making wise the simple, giving joy to the heart, giving light to the eyes, enduring forever, and all of them are righteous.

These verses remind us that God's Word is primarily about *transformation*. It reveals to us not a generic God, but the specific truth about the Lord's character, mission, and will. Scripture is God's road map for the journey of life. To live faithfully as God's missional people we need to breathe in and out Scripture on a daily basis. It is our fuel.

The six-fold recurring pattern of verses 7–9 reminds us of God's six days of creative activity. The implication is that Scripture is complete. It teaches us the truth about the Lord. Note also that "Lord" is now used rather that "God." With the revelation of the law of the Lord comes *specificity* and *clarity* of instruction. Creation witnesses to the existence and glory of the Creator; Scripture provides us with details and direct teaching to shape us into the people whom the Lord created us to be.

Verse 10 emphasizes the *value* and *desirability* of the Lord's teaching. For those with eyes to see and ears to hear, it is more valuable than gold and more delicious and savory than the finest honey. This is because it provides us with access to the will and desires of our Creator. It is the Lord's gift to us.

1. What does Scripture teach us that nature cannot?

2. How does Psalm 19 describe the power and beauty of God's Word?

3. How would you describe the power of Scripture in your life?

FIVE

Joining Creation's Praise

Psalm 19:11–14 *By them your servant is warned; in keeping them there is great reward.* *¹²But who can discern their own errors? Forgive my hidden faults.* *¹³Keep your servant also from willful sins; may they not rule over me. Then I will be blameless, innocent of great transgression.*

¹⁴May these words of my mouth and this meditation of my heart be pleasing in your sight, LORD, *my Rock and my Redeemer.*

Key Observation. By opening ourselves up to God's cleansing work, we join with creation in praising God with our words.

Understanding the Word. Psalm 19 reaches its climax in verses 11–14. Verses 1–6 observe that the creation witnesses to the glory and awesomeness of God. But as we noted, the testimony of creation does not offer specifics regarding God's character, mission, or will. Thus, there is no human response to the witness of creation except for the awe that comes from recognizing a Creator.

Verses 7–10 record the clear and unambiguous witness of God's Word through his Law. God's Law is transformative and effective in revealing God's truth and will for humanity. It is priceless. It is a complete revelation. Just as there were six days of God's creative activity (see Genesis 1:1–31), there are six different synonyms for the Torah and six recurrences of the name the Lord. We also see how Jesus serves as the perfectly faithful human and the living Word of God for the world. Jesus reveals God through his life, death, and resurrection.

In verses 11–14, humanity responds and joins with creation in declaring the good news about God. The revelation of the Torah of the Lord creates the response in humanity. In verse 11, the psalmist recognized the power of God's Word in revealing God's way through the world. They serve both to warn God's people and to point to the way of greatest blessing. This truth overwhelmed the psalmist and caused him to recognize his lack of faithfulness and the presence of both intentional and unintentional errors in his life. In other words, the Law of the Lord speaks directly to us about our potential as God's people and our pitfalls in our struggles to love God and neighbor. What are we to do in light of recognition of our own sins and lack before the Lord? This psalm has good news. We turn to God and pray for cleansing (vv. 12–13).

God hears our prayers. Psalm 19 assumes transformation and ends powerfully. Verse 14 testifies of the Lord's work in the life of the psalmist. He moved from awestruck observer of creation's praise (vv. 1–6) to recipient of revelation through the Law of the Lord to a person with a testimony of transformation as the psalmist's own voice joined the chorus of creation (vv. 7–10). May we experience this transformation as well so that we can join in the witness of verse 14: "May these words of my mouth and this meditation of my heart be pleasing in your sight, LORD, my Rock and my Redeemer." Note that verse 14 contains the seventh occurrence of "LORD" in the psalm. With our transformed witness, the revelation of the Lord is now complete.

This psalm is rich. It reminds us of the wonder of God's world in which we live, it revels in the power of God's Word to reveal our deepest needs, it testifies to God's willingness to forgive and transform us, and it calls us to realign with God's mission by adding our witness to the chorus of all creation.

1. What needs in the psalmist's life does the Law of the Lord reveal?

2. What is the connection between transformation and mission?

3. What is the psalmist's goal in praying Psalm 19?

WEEK FOUR

GATHERING DISCUSSION OUTLINE

A. Open session in prayer.

B. View video for this week's reading.

C. What general impressions and thoughts do you have after considering the video and reading the daily writings on these Scriptures? What specifically did this week's psalms teach you about faith, life, and prayer? What do both Psalm 8 and 19 teach us about creation and our place in it?

D. Discuss selected questions from the daily readings.

1. **KEY OBSERVATION (PSALM 8:1–2):** Praise reminds God's people of the greatness and majesty of the Lord.

   DISCUSSION QUESTION: How does Psalm 8 describe the praise of God?

2. **KEY OBSERVATION (PSALM 8:3–9):** God created humanity as the climax of creation; Jesus models this way of life for us.

   DISCUSSION QUESTION: What does Psalm 8 remind us about the role of humanity in God's creation?

3. **KEY OBSERVATION (PSALM 19:1–6):** Creation points to the Creator.

   DISCUSSION QUESTION: How does nature proclaim God's glory? What are the limitations of nature's revelation?

4. **KEY OBSERVATION (PSALM 19:7–10):** Scripture reveals the truth of creation and our need for God.

   DISCUSSION QUESTION: What does Scripture teach us that nature cannot?

5. **KEY OBSERVATION (PSALM 19:11–14):** By opening ourselves up to God's cleansing work, we join with creation in praising God with our words.

   DISCUSSION QUESTION: What is the connection between transformation and mission?

E. Close session with prayer.

WEEK FIVE

Psalms 11–15

Security and Justice

INTRODUCTION

As we begin our fifth week of study, let us review our journey. The Psalms are God's gift to his people. They serve to give voice to our prayers. The book of Psalms is unique in the Scriptures in the sense that the prayers of God's people become the Word of God for later generations of God's people.

As we have already experienced, the Psalms cover a wide swath of human experience. The opening and closing Psalms (1–2 and 146–150) provide a foundation for reading the rest of the Psalter. The life of faith is a journey. The Lord called Israel to serve as a missional people who embodied God's holy character for all creation and all nations (see Genesis 12:3 and Exodus 19:4–6). This call remains the vocation and mission of Jesus' followers today (see Matthew 4:17–22 and 1 Peter 2:9). When we follow Jesus into the world on mission, we will discover the true power and purpose of the Psalms. They give voice to our joys, our deepest longings, our gratitude, and our trusting reliance on God. As we anticipate the joy and praise of New Creation (Psalms 146–150), we stay rooted in Scripture and the assurance that God has secured the future.

Of course, this orientation does not make us immune to the challenges of living a life of faithfulness in the world. There will be times of persecution, failure, and hardship. There will be moments of joy and peace. The Psalms teach us how to live in the *now* of our lives by teaching us to pray without ceasing in all circumstances.

Psalms 11–15 continue this journey. With the exception of Psalm 8, Psalms 3–10 are all laments.

Psalm 11 introduces us to a new type of prayer: the psalm of trust. Psalm 11 affirms the pray-er's reliance on the trustworthiness of God as key to the life of faith.

Psalms 12–13 offer laments related to the ongoing presence of evil and evildoers in the world. These psalms ask for God's sustaining help due to the challenges of living for God in a world that does not yet acknowledge or worship the Lord. These prayers are always timely as God's people can find themselves troubled by the news headlines of the day. These psalms witness that there is a way through the world for those who trust God.

Psalm 14 is another psalm of trust that, combined with Psalm 11, frames the laments of Psalm 12–13. Faithfulness is possible because God protects the righteous.

Psalm 15 is a psalm of instruction. It reminds God's people of the centrality of a God-shaped character. God's people may live in a world that lacks holiness, but it is vital for the sake of God's mission for God's people to embody the character of the God who saved them and continues to sustain them.

ONE
Trust and Security

Psalm 11 *In the* LORD *I take refuge. How then can you say to me: "Flee like a bird to your mountain.* ²*For look, the wicked bend their bows; they set their arrows against the strings to shoot from the shadows at the upright in heart.* ³*When the foundations are being destroyed, what can the righteous do?"*

⁴*The* LORD *is in his holy temple; the* LORD *is on his heavenly throne. He observes everyone on earth; his eyes examine them.* ⁵*The* LORD *examines the righteous, but the wicked, those who love violence, he hates with a passion.* ⁶*On the wicked he will rain fiery coals and burning sulfur; a scorching wind will be their lot.*

⁷*For the* LORD *is righteous, he loves justice; the upright will see his face.*

Key Observation. Trusting the Lord moment by moment is the means of finding the deepest security for living in the present.

Understanding the Word. Psalm 11 is a song of trust. It reminds God's people of the true source of their security. This is a crucial word for us today. It is easy for us to misplace our security. Too often we rely on our own strengths and resources. This may involve our wealth, our relationships, our network, our possessions, our intellect, or our talents. Psalm 11 assumes that the challenges facing God's people are more than our own assets can overcome.

Psalm 11 is divided into two parts. Verses 1–3 describe the challenges facing the faithful in the world as it exists today. Verses 4–7 proclaim a security that transcends the dangers of the present. It affirms the deep relationship between the Lord and the people of God.

Verse 1 opens with the psalmist declaring full trust in the Lord. It is in the Lord alone that the psalmist has found refuge. This was the grounding for the psalmist's life. The psalmist could face the challenges and even dangers of his present because of the Lord.

Verses 1–3 contain the problem that the psalmist's trust and faithfulness answers. The psalmist addressed the *real* concern of the community. How could the righteous find security when people with wicked or evil intent threatened their lives and families? This is no mere hypothetical question for many believers around the world today. A life of faith and mission can be risky. The psalmist's community pondered the need to flee from the dangers of the world by heading to the mountains. What are the people of God to do when it seems as if all of their assumptions and practices of how to live seem to crumble?

The psalmist knew the answer to his implied question. Security is found in the Lord. Verse 4 grounds this is the dynamic truth of the Lord's presence in our world and transcendence over all creation. As Christians, we can find comfort and peace in the reality that God is present with us in the *now* of our lives yet simultaneously able to rule with a view from all eternity.

On basis of this truth, the psalmist sketched out the implications for our lives. As we've seen in other psalms, there are two groups of people: the righteous and the wicked. The psalmist assumed that he is among the righteous. Whenever we find these divisions in Scripture, it is crucial for us to recognize that it is the Lord who makes these categories and it is the Lord who makes these judgments. As we read verses 5–6, observe that the righteous do not rejoice at the downfall of the wicked. The backdrop of the psalm is the suffering, affliction, and hardship of the righteous. Verses 5–6 describe the reversal that will ultimately occur if those who prefer and practice injustice and violence do not turn from their ways to abide in the Lord. Verse 7 reminds God's people of their hope-filled future. The takeaway is that God's people must stay on course in the present and model God's holy character with the assurance that this is the right way to make it through the world.

1. What are you facing today that challenges your trust in God?

2. What practices do you keep that ground you in God?

3. What kind of person does Psalm 11 invite you to become so that you are able to live with integrity as one of the righteous?

TWO

Dependence on the Lord

Psalm 12 *Help, L*ORD*, for no one is faithful anymore; those who are loyal have vanished from the human race.* *²Everyone lies to their neighbor; they flatter with their lips but harbor deception in their hearts.*

*³May the L*ORD *silence all flattering lips and every boastful tongue—⁴those who say, "By our tongues we will prevail; our own lips will defend us—who is lord over us?"*

*⁵"Because the poor are plundered and the needy groan, I will now arise," says the L*ORD*. "I will protect them from those who malign them." ⁶And the words of the L*ORD *are flawless, like silver purified in a crucible, like gold refined seven times.*

*⁷You, L*ORD*, will keep the needy safe and will protect us forever from the wicked, ⁸who freely strut about when what is vile is honored by the human race.*

Key Observation. The Lord cares about and protects the poor and needy from those who claim self-reliance and self-determinism.

Understanding the Word. The life of faithfulness is challenging. The world that we live in is complex. The issues of the day can be daunting. This psalm explores the isolation that God's people can experience when they forget their foundation.

Verse 1 opens with a cry for help directed to the Lord. This is the Hebrew word *hosanna* that readers may recognize from the gospel story of Jesus' entry into Jerusalem on Palm Sunday. *Hosanna* means "save." Thus it is more than just calling for help. The psalmist recognizes that it is the Lord alone to whom he can turn.

What is the reason for this call? The psalmist felt as though he was utterly alone in attempting to walk faithfully with the Lord. In verses 1–2 the psalmist exclaimed his belief that all of the faithful have vanished. There was no one who remained loyally committed to the ways of God. In fact, the psalmist declared that everyone spoke deceptively and plotted ill. Have you ever felt this way? How do we pray when it seems as though we are the only ones who trust the Lord and care about his mission?

Verses 3–4 add specifics to the psalmist's plea for help. The psalmist felt oppressed. The psalmist asked the Lord to silence all who were using their voices for deceitfulness and boasting about their own power. Life confronts us with choices and differing philosophies. One subtle temptation involves the myth of self-reliance. We can deny the existence of God and power of our own faith by acting as if it is our talents and strength alone that determine our destiny. The psalmist recognized his true need for God and was overwhelmed by a society in which this truth was denied. When self-reliance is overemphasized, we find a society shaped by selfishness and injustice. We treat resources as limited and hoard them for our own use or for the use of those whom we love. This psalmist was on the short end of this type of world.

The psalmist then shared the Lord's response. The Lord is not for the self-reliant, but for *justice*. The Lord rises up to protect the poor and needy against those who claim self-reliance and self-determinism as their philosophy of life.

Verses 6–8 affirm the psalmist's trust and confidence in the Lord's care and protection. Unlike the wicked whose words are fickle and deceptive, the words of the Lord are sure and secure. They are like the purest silver or gold. They are money in the bank. Therefore, the psalmist *knew* that his life was safe. Regardless of how desperate the situation appears in the moment, the Lord safeguards those who truly recognize their need for God. This psalm reminds us that the Lord is present for those who are desperate for what only God can do. O, that we would all live out of this sort of dependence!

1. What is the problem that confronts the psalmist in Psalm 12?

2. How did the Lord answer the psalmist?

3. What warning does Psalm 12 offer to us regarding self-reliance?

THREE
Faith in Times of Silence

Psalm 13 *How long, L*ORD*? Will you forget me forever? How long will you hide your face from me?* *²How long must I wrestle with my thoughts and day after day have sorrow in my heart? How long will my enemy triumph over me?*

*³Look on me and answer, L*ORD *my God. Give light to my eyes, or I will sleep in death,* *⁴and my enemy will say, "I have overcome him," and my foes will rejoice when I fall.*

⁵But I trust in your unfailing love; my heart rejoices in your salvation. *⁶I will sing the L*ORD*'s praise, for he has been good to me.*

Key Observation. Times of suffering and perceived silence by God can serve as opportunities for deepening faith.

Understanding the Word. Psalm 13 serves as a model lament in terms of its directness and simplicity. Its six verses divide neatly into three parts: verses 1–2 (complaint), verses 3–4 (petition), and verses 5–6 (statement of faith). Psalm 13 is the prayer of an individual who desperately needs God to act.

In verses 1–2, the question "How long?" repeats four times. This heightens the desperation of the psalmist's prayer and emphasizes his dire need for the Lord to act. It is clear that the psalmist was suffering deep anguish due to a perceived separation from God and an unspecified action by an enemy.

Our psalm assumes a deep relationship between the psalmist and the Lord. The psalmist did not understand the absence of God when he needed him the most. How can the God whom he served faithfully not show up? Sometimes the very faith that we profess can make a difficult trial worse because we can suffer a crisis of faith in addition to having to deal with the trauma of the moment. The psalmist ached internally in the silence of God's inaction while also feeling humiliated at the hands of his enemy.

What do we do in such situations? The temptation may be to change course and seek help in another person or philosophy. But the psalmist remained steadfast. The psalmist turned up the volume of his prayer. Verses 3–4 put all of the psalmist's future hope in the hands of the Lord.

Hardships and trials challenge our faith. They cut through our shallow sayings and call us to a renewed and vigorous faith. The psalmist laid out his situation and called the Lord to act. He addresses God as "LORD my God" (v. 3). He may have felt as though God was not paying attention to him or that God had withdrawn favor, but the Lord remained *his* God. He prayed out of this sense of relational certainty. He knew God and trusted that he would be faithful. Notice that verses 3–4 contain the same core issues of complaint from verses 1–2: the perceived absence of God and the threat of an external enemy. The psalmist directly addressed both. He needed God to act in the present or he would die and his adversary would gloat in victory.

The tone of the psalm changes dramatically in verses 5–6. The psalmist had shared his heart. His needs and frustrations were in the open. Now the psalmist was ready to live again. We don't know the final outcome of the prayers, but the psalmist moved forward in renewed hope and purpose. Verse 5 affirms the psalmist's faith. He prayed emphatically: *I* trust in God's steadfast/loyal love and rejoice in God's ability to deliver. Come what may, I will live in this truth. Verse six closes the prayer with a vow. The psalmist anticipated God's answer and affirmed his intention to sing to the Lord for the good outcome that the psalmist would enjoy.

1. How does Psalm 13 teach us to pray when it seems as though God is not listening to us?

2. What can we learn about faith in the face of adversity from Psalm 13?

3. What would your life look like if you decided to trust God fully with your life, your family, and your future?

FOUR

Loving Justice

Psalm 14: *The fool says in his heart, "There is no God." They are corrupt, their deeds are vile; there is no one who does good.*

²The LORD looks down from heaven on all mankind to see if there are any who understand, any who seek God. ³All have turned away, all have become corrupt; there is no one who does good, not even one.

⁴Do all these evildoers know nothing?
They devour my people as though eating bread; they never call on the Lord.
⁵But there they are, overwhelmed with dread, for God is present in the company
of the righteous. ⁶You evildoers frustrate the plans of the poor, but the Lord *is*
their refuge.

⁷Oh, that salvation for Israel would come out of Zion! When the Lord
restores his people, let Jacob rejoice and Israel be glad!

Key Observation. Justice and love for humanity and creation flows out of our
love for the Lord.

Understanding the Word. Psalm 14 is a powerful testimony to the chaos of
our world when the Lord is not at the center of humanity's intentions. The core
of Israel's ethic is the love of God and neighbor. God transforms his people to
embody this love in community for the sake of the surrounding nations and
for the glory of the Lord.

Scripture intimately links love for God and neighbor. One cannot love God
and practice injustice to others. Justice and love for humanity and creation flows
out of our love for the Lord. This reality is the problem presented in Psalm 14.
It opens memorably, "The fool says in his heart, 'There is no God'" (v. 1). In
the Bible, the fool is the opposite of a wise person who trusts God and walks in
God's ways. The fool in Psalm 14 is not an atheist. To say, "There is no God," is
a denial that the Lord acts in our world or cares about how we live. The focus is
on the motives and intention of the fool. The fool's motivation arises from his
heart or will. The fool, by acting as if there is no God who is active in the world,
puts his own cares, desires, and wants above God's vision of justice. Thus, the
psalmist summarized his life as one who is vile and not able to act for the good.

Verses 2–6 describe the Lord's response to those who live their lives as if
God is incapable or unwilling to act. Verses 2–4 summarize the general lostness
of humanity apart from the ways of the Lord. These verses paint a pessimistic
but important portrait of our world apart from God's grace. We do not have
to look far to see the brokenness and pain that human decisions cause. The
apostle Paul in his letter to the Romans (3:10–12) quoted from Psalm 14:2–3
in his argument that culminates in the declaration, "for all have sinned and fall
short of the glory of God" (3:23).

In the midst of this, it is important to note that the Lord is seeking persons who will turn to him (v. 2). God desires to see justice and abundance prevail over all the earth. Verse 4 suggests that the choice of evil is irrational. How can humanity not *know* the living God? God seems surprised in this psalm. Why choose to act in ways contrary to the beautiful designs that God has for his world and people?

Yet, much of humanity does choose to live in opposition to God's reign. Verses 4–6 describe this in terms of the foolish and wicked oppressing God's people. Here God's people find themselves among the poor and marginalized. However, Psalm 14 affirms that God is with the *marginalized* and serves as their protector and refuge.

Verse 7 proclaims the Lord's salvation. The psalmist, in a statement of trust, called for God's people to rejoice in anticipation of the Lord's full restoration of justice and righteousness.

1. What does it mean to be a fool according to Psalm 14?

2. How did the psalmist describe the essential problem facing humanity? Do you agree or disagree?

3. How does Psalm 14 invite us to trust God more deeply?

FIVE

Love for God and Neighbor

Psalm 15 *LORD, who may dwell in your sacred tent? Who may live on your holy mountain?*

²The one whose walk is blameless, who does what is righteous, who speaks the truth from their heart; ³whose tongue utters no slander, who does no wrong to a neighbor, and casts no slur on others; ⁴who despises a vile person but honors those who fear the LORD; who keeps an oath even when it hurts, and does not change their mind; ⁵who lends money to the poor without interest; who does not accept a bribe against the innocent.

Whoever does these things will never be shaken.

Key Observation. Our love for God must manifest in our relationships with all people.

Understanding the Word. This week we've explored two psalms of trust (11 and 14) and two laments (12–13). All four psalms explored the struggle of living for the Lord in a world that does not acknowledge God's kingdom. God's people can face oppression and injustice by persons who live by their own rules rather than embodying justice and righteousness.

These psalms testify to an unwavering trust in the Lord. Despite hardships, these prayers witness to a dogged and rich faith that can guide us on our journey as God's missional people. Yet there is a subtle temptation when the wicked appear to prevail in the present. The temptation is to lower our standards, maybe just a little, to perhaps lessen the cost of a life of faithfulness. Enter Psalm 15. Psalm 15 instructs God's people in the habits of those committed to holy living in an unholy world.

Psalm 15 served originally as a liturgy for entering into the temple in Jerusalem. It connects love for God with love for neighbor. If the journey of faith ends in the praise and adoration of the Lord and his victory (Psalms 146–150), this psalm reminds us of the importance of personal holiness and character as we live in anticipation of God's future abundance.

Psalm 15 unpacks as a general question (v. 1) followed by a detailed answer (vv. 2–5). Verse 5 concludes with a powerful promise.

Verse 1 opens the psalm by asking the Lord for the characteristics of a person who may enter into God's presence. Psalm 15 does not set admissions requirements for a relationship with God. It is describing the lifestyle of a person who has received God's grace. Psalm 15 invites us to answer a similar question today: What kind of person do I need to become in light of the grace and kindness that I've received from God in Jesus Christ?

The Lord's answer to this question may seem surprising as it lacks any *religious* acts. For example, there are no references to Sabbath or sacrifices. Instead, verses 2–5 focus on how we relate and treat others. In other words, it suggests that our love for God must manifest in our relationships with all people and especially with God's people. Observe that there are ten lines of instruction in these verses. This is intentional. Just as there are Ten Commandments from Sinai (see Exodus 20:2–17; cf. Deuteronomy 5:6–21), Psalm 15 offers ten lines of ethical instruction to guide the godly in their walk with the Lord.

These verses focus on practicing faithfulness in our relationships with others. This is the meaning of a blameless walk and right action. This involves speaking truthfully and not using our speech to injure others (vv. 2–3). The holy life also means honoring God's people rather than giving special privileges to those who reject God (v. 4). People also honor God by keeping their word (v. 4). The blameless life also manifests in blessing the poor with no-interest loans and refusing bribes against someone who is innocent (v. 5). Some of these practices may be costly in terms of money, loss of prestige in the eyes of the world, or crossing someone powerful. Yet it is in these acts of integrity that our holiness sets us apart from the ways of the world and points others to the ways of the Lord.

God calls us to live this way counterculturally as an abiding witness to God's mission and kingdom. Verse 5 promises that faithfulness has its reward: security for all eternity.

1. What kind of person does Psalm 15 invite you to become?

2. What is the most challenging part of Psalm 15 for you to live out?

3. What role does faithful service to your neighbors and to the poor play in your life as a follower of Jesus?

WEEK FIVE

GATHERING DISCUSSION OUTLINE

A. Open session in prayer.

B. View video for this week's reading.

C. What general impressions and thoughts do you have after considering the video and reading the daily writings on these Scriptures? What specifically did this week's psalms teach you about faith, life, and prayer?

D. Discuss selected questions from the daily readings.

1. **KEY OBSERVATION (PSALM 11):** Trusting the Lord moment by moment is the means of finding the deepest security for living in the present.

   DISCUSSION QUESTION: What kind of person does this psalm invite you to become to be able to live with integrity as one of the righteous?

2. **KEY OBSERVATION (PSALM 12):** The Lord cares about and protects the poor and needy from those who claim self-reliance and self-determinism.

   DISCUSSION QUESTION: What warning does this psalm offer to use regarding self-reliance?

3. **KEY OBSERVATION (PSALM 13):** Times of suffering and perceived silence by God can serve as opportunities for deepening faith.

   DISCUSSION QUESTION: How does Psalm 13 teach us to pray when it seems as though God is not listening to us?

4.   **KEY OBSERVATION (PSALM 14):** Justice and love for humanity and creation flows out of our love for the Lord.

   DISCUSSION QUESTION: How does the psalmist describe the essential problem facing humanity?

5.   **KEY OBSERVATION (PSALM 15):** Our love for God must manifest in our relationships with all people.

   DISCUSSION QUESTION: What role does faithful service to your neighbors and to the poor play in your life as a follower of Jesus?

E.   Close session with prayer.

WEEK SIX

Psalms 16–18

Security and the Messiah

INTRODUCTION

Psalms 16–18 continue the theme of security in a world where God's people find themselves surrounded and oppressed by enemies. Last week, we read through two psalms of trust (Psalms 11 and 14), two laments asking for God's help with enemies (Psalms 12–13), and a psalm of instruction about the character necessary to enjoy the presence of God (Psalm 15).

Psalms 16 and 17 are prayers for protection from enemies. In each of these prayers, the psalmist is adamant about his innocence. He recognizes that true security can be found in the Lord alone and commits to a way of life in which the Lord serves as his refuge from the dangers and snares of those who act against the mission of God through injustice and violence. These psalms will help us to examine our notions of security. They will equip us to pray wisely when we feel insecure. These prayers assume that living faithfully as God's people does not make us immune to the ill intentions of those who do not share our faith commitments. They remind us that seeking security in any person or thing other than God is a dead end. God is trustworthy and invites us into his presence to find refuge from the world as we seek to live as his witnesses.

Psalm 18 is one of the longest in the book of Psalms. It is a royal psalm that focuses on celebrating and giving thanks for a great victory that the Lord has won for his messiah. Since this psalm is about the Davidic king, it functions as a messianic psalm that finds its richest fulfillment in the life, death, and resurrection of Jesus the Messiah. Psalm 18 focuses our ideas of security onto the Messiah who models faithfulness and whom God delivers from the realm of death and chaos.

This week's readings will help us to grow in our ability to live boldly for God in the world by finding our surest foundation in the Lord and in the victory that he accomplished through the resurrection of Jesus.

ONE

Strength to Praise

Psalm 16 ESV *Preserve me, O God, for in you I take refuge. [2]I say to the LORD, "You are my LORD; I have no good apart from you."*

[3]As for the saints in the land, they are the excellent ones, in whom is all my delight. [4]The sorrows of those who run after another god shall multiply; their drink offerings of blood I will not pour out or take their names on my lips.

[5]The LORD is my chosen portion and my cup; you hold my lot. [6]The lines have fallen for me in pleasant places; indeed, I have a beautiful inheritance.

[7]I bless the LORD who gives me counsel; in the night also my heart instructs me. [8]I have set the LORD always before me; because he is at my right hand, I shall not be shaken.

[9]Therefore my heart is glad, and my whole being rejoices; my flesh also dwells secure. [10]For you will not abandon my soul to Sheol, or let your holy one see corruption.

[11]You make known to me the path of life; in your presence there is fullness of joy; at your right hand are pleasures forevermore.

Key Observation. Trust in the Lord supplies us with the strength, hope, and witness to live a life of passionate praise and faithfulness before a watching world.

Understanding the Word. We long for security. It's part of our humanity. God created us to live in harmony with our Creator, with creation, and with one another (see Genesis 1–2). But human sin and disobedience has disrupted God's creation and sin manifests itself in broken relationships, violence, greed, and injustice. All of these lead to insecurity in our world. News organizations report a constant flow of natural disasters, financial crises, and conflicts. Yet in the midst of this, as God's people, we seek to represent hope and serve as agents of blessing for the sake of God's mission to the nations. Psalm 16 helps us to pray when we experience insecurity. Its words are important as they remind God's people that true security is found only in the Lord. Others may promise it, but only the Lord delivers.

Psalm 16 divides into two parts: verses 1–6 and 7–11. Part one opens with a plea and a commitment. The psalmist exclaimed his desire to take refuge in the Lord and asked God to provide security.

Verses 2–6 put flesh to the psalmist's vow of commitment. The psalmist was not hedging his bet by pursuing multiple security options. This is often our tactic in the modern world. We opt for God and [fill in the blank] as the key to making it through the world. For the psalmist, the Lord was the only *Lord* and only source of true goodness (v. 2). In other words, the psalmist was "all in" in terms of commitment.

In verses 3–6 the psalmist described his commitment to God as his Lord by aligning himself with God's people (v. 3), proclaiming the futility of trusting in other gods (v. 4), and the already-experienced blessing of his relationship with the Lord (vv. 5–6).

The second half of the psalm turns to praise. These verses contain some of the most hopeful and confident statements in the Psalter. Verses 7–9 speak of the psalmist's intention to worship and sing praises to the Lord. The psalmist did this continually and remained in a vital moment-by-moment walk. This was the source of the psalmist's security. He did not merely turn to God when he encountered trouble. He remained in communion with God and listened attentively.

Peter quoted verses 8–11 during his sermon on the Day of Pentecost as an Old Testament witness to Jesus' resurrection (Acts 2:25–28). The psalmist's confidence in God ran so deep that he lived in the security that even death would not prevail over God's ability to sustain him. This is a faith that we ought to desire for ourselves. The psalmist had his mind made up and had aligned himself fully with the Lord then and for all eternity. That provided him with the strength, hope, and witness to live a life of passionate praise and faithfulness before a watching world. Do you have this security in your life?

1. How would you live differently if you had the confidence of the psalmist?

2. What challenges in your life bring you insecurity?

3. How does Psalm 16 teach you to abide in the Lord's security?

TWO

Faith and Times of Trouble

Psalm 17 ESV *Hear a just cause, O Lord; attend to my cry! Give ear to my prayer from lips free of deceit! ²From your presence let my vindication come! Let your eyes behold the right!*

³You have tried my heart, you have visited me by night, you have tested me, and you will find nothing; I have purposed that my mouth will not transgress. ⁴With regard to the works of man, by the word of your lips I have avoided the ways of the violent. ⁵My steps have held fast to your paths; my feet have not slipped.

⁶I call upon you, for you will answer me, O God; incline your ear to me; hear my words. ⁷Wondrously show your steadfast love, O Savior of those who seek refuge from their adversaries at your right hand.

⁸Keep me as the apple of your eye; hide me in the shadow of your wings, ⁹from the wicked who do me violence, my deadly enemies who surround me.

¹⁰They close their hearts to pity; with their mouths they speak arrogantly. ¹¹They have now surrounded our steps; they set their eyes to cast us to the ground. ¹²He is like a lion eager to tear, as a young lion lurking in ambush.

¹³Arise, O Lord! Confront him, subdue him! Deliver my soul from the wicked by your sword, ¹⁴from men by your hand, O Lord, from men of the world whose portion is in this life. You fill their womb with treasure; they are satisfied with children, and they leave their abundance to their infants.

¹⁵As for me, I shall behold your face in righteousness; when I awake, I shall be satisfied with your likeness.

Key Observation. The life of faith does not make us immune to the troubles of life or the accusations of others.

Understanding the Word. Living faithfully and practicing justice does not guarantee an easy pathway through life. Psalm 17 is a prayer for those times when we've done the right thing and still find ourselves neck-deep in trouble. The psalmist pled for help from the Lord by stating his innocence (vv. 1–5), appealing for God to act (vv. 6–12), and making a final request for vindication (vv. 13–15).

The psalmist was adamant about his innocence and need for God's help in verse 1. The psalmist was bold in his language. We often hesitate to put forward our own innocence, but the psalmist had no qualms. He knew that he had acted justly and rightly; he also believed that he was being treated unjustly. In verses 2–5, he invited the Lord to examine his life and then make the bad situation right for him. The psalmist denied that he had intended or planned any evil. He had avoided talk or speech that injured others. He refused to take bribes. Instead, the psalmist had walked in God's ways. He had kept the Lord's commandments. Recall the words of Psalm 1 and its exhortation to avoid evil through a steady and consistent diet of the Lord's instruction. The psalmist had done this.

In the psalmist's mind, there was only one obvious outcome: God must act. As we work through this text, allow God to show you your own heart. What kind of a person do you need to become to pray this kind of prayer with integrity?

Having demonstrated his innocence, the psalmist made specific appeals to the Lord to act (vv. 6–12). He repeated his opening call for God to listen (v. 6). Then the psalmist asked God to put his wondrous steadfast and loyal love into action (v. 7). *Love* is a core attribute of the Lord (see Exodus 34:6). This love is directly at the heart of the relationship between the Lord and his people. It is a loyal and faithful commitment. The psalmist appealed to God's love because he steadfastly believed that he had held up his end of the relationship. The psalmist was desperate for God to use his saving powers to protect him from the enemies who afflict him.

In verse 8, we discover that the psalmist was either in the temple or visualizing it. To hide in the "shadow of your wings" is temple image of a pray-er bowing before the wings of the golden cherubim who sit on the edges of the ark of the covenant in the holiest part of the temple. The glory of the Lord hovered between them. In other words, the psalmist sought refuge in the presence of God. Only God could save the psalmist due to the overwhelming danger of the psalmist's foes (vv. 9–12).

The psalmist ended his prayer with a final plea for help and a statement of trust and belief that God would indeed answer him (vv. 13–15).

1. How does Psalm 17 challenge you to live so that you may be able to assert your blamelessness as the psalmist did?

2. What daily practices do you keep that help you to live a life of faithfulness?

3. Is there anything in your life that is keeping you from trusting the Lord fully today? What would it mean for you to let go of these things?

THREE

Hope for the Messiah

Psalm 18:1–6 *I love you, Lord, my strength.*

²The Lord is my rock, my fortress and my deliverer; my God is my rock, in whom I take refuge, my shield and the horn of my salvation, my stronghold.

³I called to the Lord, who is worthy of praise, and I have been saved from my enemies. ⁴The cords of death entangled me; the torrents of destruction overwhelmed me. ⁵The cords of the grave coiled around me; the snares of death confronted me.

⁶In my distress I called to the Lord; I cried to my God for help. From his temple he heard my voice; my cry came before him, into his ears.

Key Observation. The hope for Messiah in the Psalms reaches its climax in the death and resurrection of Jesus.

Understanding the Word. Psalm 18 is the third longest psalm after Psalm 78 and 119. Psalm 18 focuses on the victory that God gives to Israel's king. Like Psalm 2, it is a royal psalm. This means that it was originally written as a psalm for use in the celebration of David or one of his descendants. Royal psalms offer a tangible worldly focus for the *security* that God's people desire as they seek to walk faithfully through the world. From our previous reading of Psalm 2 and Psalm 146, we know that the book of Psalms makes two related moves regarding human kingship.

First, the book of Psalms was organized for worship after Israel's exile to Babylon and return to the land. Historically, this meant that Israel did not have its own king. Post-exile, the Persians, Greeks, and Romans ruled over God's people from 538 BC onward. The only exception was the brief period following the Maccabean revolt (142–63 BC) when God's people enjoyed self-rule. Thus, when Israel prayed and sang the royal psalms, they were asking the Lord to restore the Davidic king. These psalms served as longings for the coming of God's Messiah who would renew God's kingdom and guide God's people in faithfulness.

Second, the psalms offer a critique of human leadership. We saw in our reading of Psalm 146 that it warns against trusting in any human leader. The Lord is the true King.

As Christians, these two elements—a longing for the Messiah and distrust of human leaders—find a powerful resolution in the life, death, and resurrection of Jesus the Messiah. Jesus is the long-awaited son of David, and he is also God. Thus, as followers of Jesus, we read Israel's royal psalms as prayers and praises to God for the victory over sin, injustice, oppression, and evil that he offers to all who trust and follow Jesus.

As you read through Psalm 18, you will notice that it is written through the eyes and experiences of Israel's king. When later readers of the psalm prayed these words, they were using them not to remember a past king, but as a means of praying for God's future king or Messiah. *Messiah* means "anointed one." All of Israel's kings were anointed at their consecration as king. In 587 BC, the Babylonians destroyed Jerusalem and ended the reign of David and his descendants. Yet God's people never gave up hope. They longed for God to renew his kingdom by sending a new Messiah to rule over them. The New Testament announces that this new king was Jesus Christ. *Christ* means "Messiah."

In verses 1–19, the king gave thanks to the Lord for leading him to victory. We'll focus on verse 1–6 for today's lesson.

Verses 1–3 praise the Lord with rich and dynamic language. These lines have inspired countless hymns and contemporary praise songs that God's people use to this day. The previous two psalms (Psalms 16–17) focused on God as a refuge. These verses give us words to describe what this means. The Lord is a rock, a fortress, a shield, a deliverer, and the horn of salvation. The Lord was worthy to be praised because the psalmist had experienced the power of God's salvation. This is not a lament; this is the testimony of answered prayer. The Lord is a refuge because he is the God who *saves*.

Verses 4–6 describe the psalmist's previous condition as truly desperate. He was trapped in death. The waters of the underworld ensnared him. When we think of this psalm as ultimately praise for the life, death, and resurrection of Jesus, we can read verses 1–6 as a declaration of the victory that the Lord rendered through Jesus' death and resurrection. Jesus died on the cross, but

God vindicated him by raising him triumphantly from the grave. This is the true ground for our security.

1. How do the opening six verses of Psalm 18 teach us to give thanks and praise to the Lord?

2. What are some areas in your life for which you can give thanks to God today?

3. How does Psalm 18:1–6 teach us to praise God for the death and resurrection of Jesus?

FOUR

No Problem Is Bigger Than God

Psalm 18:7–24 *The earth trembled and quaked, and the foundations of the mountains shook; they trembled because he was angry. ⁸Smoke rose from his nostrils; consuming fire came from his mouth, burning coals blazed out of it. ⁹He parted the heavens and came down; dark clouds were under his feet. ¹⁰He mounted the cherubim and flew; he soared on the wings of the wind. ¹¹He made darkness his covering, his canopy around him—the dark rain clouds of the sky. ¹²Out of the brightness of his presence clouds advanced, with hailstones and bolts of lightning. ¹³The LORD thundered from heaven; the voice of the Most High resounded. ¹⁴He shot his arrows and scattered the enemy, with great bolts of lightning he routed them. ¹⁵The valleys of the sea were exposed and the foundations of the earth laid bare at your rebuke, LORD, at the blast of breath from your nostrils.*

¹⁶He reached down from on high and took hold of me; he drew me out of deep waters. ¹⁷He rescued me from my powerful enemy, from my foes, who were too strong for me. ¹⁸They confronted me in the day of my disaster, but the Lord was my support. ¹⁹He brought me out into a spacious place; he rescued me because he delighted in me.

²⁰The Lord has dealt with me according to my righteousness; according to the cleanness of my hands he has rewarded me. ²¹For I have kept the ways of the Lord; I am not guilty of turning from my God. ²²All his laws are before me; I have not turned away from his decrees. ²³I have been blameless before him and have kept myself from sin. ²⁴The Lord has rewarded me according to my righteousness, according to the cleanness of my hands in his sight.

Key Observation. There is no problem that is beyond the redemptive power of God.

Understanding the Word. In verses 7–19, the psalmist used creational and mythic imagery to describe the victory of God. This part of the psalm helps us to understand that God's victory was a cosmic and world-shaping action. It was not merely about rescue of the Messiah. God's actions secured the very creation and future for the Messiah and for the people of God.

This section of the psalm is difficult to understand because it uses language that belongs to the ancient world and its belief system. When the ancients talked about creation, their focus was not on the beginnings of the universe (this is a *modern* conversation) but on how the gods fought for supremacy and secured the earth against the forces that threated the destruction of the world. In this part of the psalm, God's messiah, was giving thanks to the Lord for saving him. The Lord has the power to save because the Lord is the Creator of the cosmos.

Verse 7 names some of the most awe-inspiring parts of nature: the earth itself and the foundations of the highest mountains. We feel puny in comparison to these. Yet they *trembled, quaked,* and *shook* before the Lord due to God's anger at the injustice experienced by God's messiah.

The Lord's anger in verses 7–14 is described in terms of a raging story. This is the language of creation. The waters of chaos and death trap God's messiah (vv. 4–5). The Lord roars out of heaven in the form of a thunderstorm. All creation quakes as God approaches with lightning, thunder, and hail. The Lord is so powerful that he uses the most fearsome parts of creation as a tool to bring about the deliverance of the king.

As we saw in verses 4–5, the waters of chaos and death had pulled the king under. He was trapped and helpless. The future looked bleak. God's mission seemed lost. But the Lord of creation cannot be defeated by any power no matter how insurmountable it may be to mere humans. This psalm reminds us that there is nothing in our lives beyond the capacity of God to redeem. Verses 15–19 detail the Lord's salvation of the messiah. Just as God delivered his people from Egypt by splitting the Red Sea and guiding them to safety, the

Lord exposed the foundations of the world and the depths of the waters of death and chaos (vv. 15–16; cf. Exodus 15:8). The Lord rescued the Messiah and restored him to abundance.

After telling the story of God's dramatic and cosmic deliverance, the Messiah declared his life of faithfulness as a model to be followed. The Messiah practiced justice and obedience to the Lord. He was faithful to act rightly in all of his relationships. (This is the meaning of "righteousness.") Jesus fulfilled this role perfectly as long-awaited Messiah. Through his faithfulness, God accomplished his victory over injustice, sin, and death.

1. How does Psalm 18 help us understand the power of the Lord to save?

2. How does this psalm connect the Messiah's righteousness with the salvation of the Lord?

3. What challenges in your life seem overwhelming? How do the words of Psalm 18 bring you comfort?

FIVE

Responding with Gratitude

Psalm 18:25–50 ESV *With the merciful you show yourself merciful; with the blameless man you show yourself blameless; ²⁶with the purified you show yourself pure; and with the crooked you make yourself seem tortuous. ²⁷For you save a humble people, but the haughty eyes you bring down. ²⁸For it is you who light my lamp; the Lord my God lightens my darkness. ²⁹For by you I can run against a troop, and by my God I can leap over a wall. ³⁰This God—his way is perfect; the word of the Lord proves true; he is a shield for all those who take refuge in him.*

³¹For who is God, but the Lord? And who is a rock, except our God?—³²the God who equipped me with strength and made my way blameless. ³³He made my feet like the feet of a deer and set me secure on the heights. ³⁴He trains my hands for war, so that my arms can bend a bow of bronze. ³⁵You have given me the shield of your salvation, and your right hand supported me, and your gentleness made me great. ³⁶You gave a wide place for my steps under me, and my feet did not slip. ³⁷I pursued my enemies and overtook them, and did not turn back till they were consumed. ³⁸I thrust them through, so that they were not able to

rise; they fell under my feet. ³⁹For you equipped me with strength for the battle; you made those who rise against me sink under me. ⁴⁰You made my enemies turn their backs to me, and those who hated me I destroyed. ⁴¹They cried for help, but there was none to save; they cried to the LORD, but he did not answer them. ⁴²I beat them fine as dust before the wind; I cast them out like the mire of the streets. ⁴³You delivered me from strife with the people; you made me the head of the nations; people whom I had not known served me. ⁴⁴As soon as they heard of me they obeyed me; foreigners came cringing to me. ⁴⁵Foreigners lost heart and came trembling out of their fortresses.

⁴⁶The LORD lives, and blessed be my rock, and exalted be the God of my salvation—⁴⁷the God who gave me vengeance and subdued peoples under me, ⁴⁸who delivered me from my enemies; yes, you exalted me above those who rose against me; you rescued me from the man of violence.

⁴⁹For this I will praise you, O LORD, among the nations, and sing to your name. ⁵⁰Great salvation he brings to his king, and shows steadfast love to his anointed, to David and his offspring forever.

Key Observation. The response to God's saving work is gratitude lived out through a life that praises and gives thanks to God.

Understanding the Word. In verses 25–45 the psalmist returned to his report of the victory that God won on his behalf. It is a mix of praise for the Lord and narrative about the salvation of the psalmist. Unlike verses 7–19, the language of verses 25–45 focuses on the psalmist's experience rather than on the creational imagery that the psalmist had used to cast God's actions into cosmic focus.

How did the psalmist describe his experience of salvation? First, in verses 25–27 he recognized that God does indeed save those who are faithful and depend fully on him to make it through the world. Those who are deviant or arrogant will not be able to stand at the end of the day.

Second, God was the source of the psalmist's strength (vv. 28–32). God empowered the psalmist with the strength and energy to complete the mission of God. This is important. God will deliver us, but as we struggle through the challenges, God will sustain us. As Paul wrote centuries later to the Corinthians about God's empowerment in times of weakness, "My grace is sufficient" (2 Cor. 12:9).

Third, the messiah was able to win an extraordinary victory because of the power and loyalty of the Lord (vv. 33–45). As you read these lines, they are militaristic and contain violent images. It is vital to recognize that it is the Lord who wins the victory. The king was merely the agent through whom God acted. These words do not justify violent acts by us or by any person of faith. They assume that the Lord's messiah was under heavy assault from the enemies of God. In the ancient world, Israel was a tiny and insignificant nation from a military perspective. If it was successful in war, it was only because of God's protection and not because of their own power or the superiority of their weapons and tactics. Most important, it is vital to remember that this psalm finds its most poignant fulfillment in the death and resurrection of Jesus the Messiah. In Jesus, God won his salvation securing victory by refusing to counter human power with any power other than love. Jesus conquered the grave because God raised his dead body from the grave to demonstrate true power and victory.

Psalm 18 reaches its climax in verses 46–50 with a final flurry of praise. Again the language is extravagant and audacious. Review the opening three verses and observe the similarities of the praise at the beginning and end of the psalm. The messiah modeled the mission of God. He praised God for his powerful acts of salvation. He was grateful for the deliverance that he had experienced. Verse 49 also keeps God's mission to bless the nations in view. Yes, God had rescued his messiah from the hand of enemies, but this deliverance shifts to be a word of witness to the world including those who had acted against the king. The Lord is *for* God's people, but this is so that God's people can serve as his hands, feet, and mouthpieces *for* the world that does not yet know and sing God's praises.

1. How do verses 25–50 of Psalm 18 teach us to praise God?

2. What is the connection between salvation and mission?

3. Who in your life needs to hear your testimony of what God has done in your life?

WEEK SIX

GATHERING DISCUSSION OUTLINE

A. Open session in prayer.

B. View video for this week's reading.

C. What general impressions and thoughts do you have after considering the video and reading the daily writings on these Scriptures? What specifically did this week's psalms teach you about faith, life, and prayer?

D. Discuss selected questions from the daily readings.

1. **KEY OBSERVATION (PSALM 16):** Trust in the Lord supplies us with the strength, hope, and witness to live a life of passionate praise and faithfulness before a watching world.

   DISCUSSION QUESTION: What challenges in your life bring you insecurity? How does this psalm teach you to abide in the Lord's security?

2. **KEY OBSERVATION (PSALM 17):** The life of faith does not make us immune to the troubles of life or the accusations of others.

   DISCUSSION QUESTION: How does Psalm 17 challenge you to live so that you may be able to assert your blamelessness as the psalmist does in Psalm 17?

3. **KEY OBSERVATION (PSALM 18:1–6):** The hope for Messiah in the Psalms reaches its climax in the death and resurrection of Jesus.

   DISCUSSION QUESTION: How does Psalm 18 teach us to praise God for the death and resurrection of Jesus?

4. **KEY OBSERVATION (PSALM 18:7–24):** There is no problem that is beyond the redemptive power of God.

   DISCUSSION QUESTION: What challenges in your life seem overwhelming? How do the words of Psalm 18 bring you comfort?

5. **KEY OBSERVATION (PSALM 18:25–50):** The response to God's saving work is gratitude lived out through a life that praises and gives thanks to God.

   DISCUSSION QUESTION: What is the connection between salvation and mission? Who in your life needs to hear your testimony of what God has done in your life?

E. Close session with prayer.

WEEK SEVEN

Psalms 20–21 and 24–25

The LORD Is King

INTRODUCTION

This week we will study two royal psalms (Psalms 20–21), a psalm about the Lord's reign (Psalm 24), and a lament (Psalm 25). We are saving two of the Psalter's most well-known psalms (Psalms 22 and 23) for an extended treatment next week.

The overall context of the Psalter is important as we reflect on the two royal psalms. Psalm 18 is a royal thanksgiving psalm and Psalm 19 is a Torah psalm. This means that in Psalms 18–21 we find three royal psalms wrapped around a psalm emphasizing the critical role of the Lord's Torah, or Law, for the life of faith. Recall that this is how the book of Psalms begins. Psalm 1 is a Torah psalm that roots the individual's happy life with a constant and steady diet of Scripture. Psalm 2 anchors the individual faithful member of God's people into God's cosmic designs by declaring that the Lord has secured the future by appointing his king to reign over his kingdom. Scripture and kingship are thus two themes that function together to serve as a prescription for God's people to live fully as God's witnesses to the world.

The Scriptures serve as our transformational instruction to shape and form us to reflect God's character. The Lord's king models faithfulness and guides God's people on mission. These themes resonate with us as Jesus' followers as Jesus modeled faithfulness to Scripture and served as God's crucified and risen Messiah. Psalms 20–21 help us to reflect on the basis for our security in the world: following and serving God's anointed one. In the Psalms, this was Israel's human king. In the New Testament, Jesus fulfills the psalmist's longing for an ideal king to restore God's kingdom. Psalm 20 focuses on praying for the

Lord to give the king success in a time of trial. Psalm 21 celebrates and gives thanks to the Lord for granting the king victory.

Our study this week then moves to Psalm 24, a powerful psalm about the Lord's kingship and our human response to it. It follows the famous Psalm 23 where the Lord is depicted as a shepherd who brings the psalmist to abide in the house of the Lord. Psalm 24 announces the Lord in all of his majesty and glory as King over all the earth. The awesomeness of the Lord's reign reminds God's people of their foundation for living.

Psalm 25 returns to lament. The psalmist prayed out of a deep trust for the Lord before crying out for help. Laments dominate the opening books of the Psalms. But lament is not the final word. The Lord who reigns over all of the earth is our anchor for life. He can be trusted and he will answer the prayers of his people. Victory is assured. The Lord has given God's people the gifts of Scripture (Torah) and the Messiah as core foundational means to moving from lament to praise.

As we read and reflect on these psalms this week, let us ponder our own journey and challenge ourselves to find our deepest security in the Lord who reigns forever and continue to follow Jesus our crucified and risen Lord into the world to make disciples. Let us do this with courage, tenacity, and prayerfully using the words of the Psalms as our guide.

ONE

God's Protection

Psalm 20 *May the LORD answer you when you are in distress; may the name of the God of Jacob protect you. ²May he send you help from the sanctuary and grant you support from Zion. ³May he remember all your sacrifices and accept your burnt offerings. ⁴May he give you the desire of your heart and make all your plans succeed. ⁵May we shout for joy over your victory and lift up our banners in the name of our God.*

May the LORD grant all your requests.

⁶Now this I know: The LORD gives victory to his anointed. He answers him from his heavenly sanctuary with the victorious power of his right hand. ⁷Some trust in chariots and some in horses, but we trust in the name of the LORD our

God. ⁸They are brought to their knees and fall, but we rise up and stand firm.
⁹Lord, give victory to the king! Answer us when we call!

Key Observation. God's kingdom is secure because of God's protection, not because of human power, weaponry, or tactics.

Understanding the Word. Psalm 20 is a royal psalm that asks for God's continued protection and support for the Lord's anointed king, or messiah, as he leads God's people in their mission to bless the nations. Psalms originally praying for the human kings appointed over God's people such as David or Solomon later became prayers for God to send a new king (Messiah) to save God's people. All psalms originally written about Israel's kings find their richest meaning as prayers for the coming of Jesus the Messiah and Savior of the world. The context is important. Psalm 18 and 21 are also royal psalms. These three royal psalms wrap around Psalm 19—a psalm that proclaims the power of the Torah. Torah and kingship are key related themes in the book of Psalms and are foundational for helping us as God's people to understand our security in God and our guide.

The king served as the Lord's agent for guiding and leading the Lord's kingdom on earth. The king was to model faithfulness to the Lord's instruction as he led God's people to embody his holy character before the nations.

Psalm 20 is a prayer for the success of the king as he defends God's people from enemies. Verses 1–5 are the petitions for the Lord's help and verses 6–9 are statements of assurance of God's help.

In verses 1–5, the king faced a trying time. The language in these verses implies that it is a time of war. In the Old Testament, Israel was a tiny nation surrounded by the superpowers of the day (usually Egypt, Assyria, Babylon, or a combination of these three). The security of Israel depended on the power of the Lord. The king presented the human agent through whom God worked. This was not a violent prayer of a militaristic society that plots to dominate its neighbors. The wars of Israel's kings were matters of self-defense in the advancement of God's ultimate mission of extending his blessings of peace and justice to the world. In our day as God's people, such a prayer is not for use in the advancement of any nation's self-interest. It is for protection for God's people, the church of Jesus, against forces that may seek to thwart its kingdom-advancing work.

The prayer of verses 1–5 recognizes that success depends fully on the Lord whose sanctuary is in Zion in Jerusalem. It is not about battle plans or weapons. The faithfulness of the king is emphasized (v. 3).

Verses 6–9 anticipate God granting the king victory. God will answer the king from the sanctuary. Again verse 7 affirms the key stance of God's people: trust in the Lord rather than gaining a false security through the best weapons developed by human inventiveness. Chariots and horses functioned as the tanks or perhaps even as the air force of the day. Those who trust merely in human tactics and military might will fall before the Lord and God's people will stand. Verse 9 ends the psalm with a final plea for the Lord's saving actions.

As we ponder this prayer for the king, let us remember our Lord and Messiah Jesus through whom God conquered the grave, the power of sin, and injustice. King Jesus was the fulfillment of the psalmist's prayer. King Jesus won God's victory through his willing submission to death on a cross rather than through wielding any type of human power or using divine privilege. He trusted the Lord. As we represent God's kingdom in our day, let us do so in the confidence that God will hear our prayers for protection and victory too.

1. What does Psalm 20 teach us about trusting the Lord for victory?

2. How does this psalm teach us to pray for protection for God's people, the church of Jesus?

3. What provides false security for us today?

TWO

Love Secures Our Future

Psalm 21 *The king rejoices in your strength, LORD. How great is his joy in the victories you give!*

²You have granted him his heart's desire and have not withheld the request of his lips. ³You came to greet him with rich blessings and placed a crown of pure gold on his head. ⁴He asked you for life, and you gave it to him—length of days, for ever and ever. ⁵Through the victories you gave, his glory is great; you have bestowed on him splendor and majesty. ⁶Surely you have granted him unending *blessings and made him glad with the joy of your presence. ⁷For the king trusts in the L*ORD*; through the unfailing love of the Most High he will not be shaken.*

*⁸Your hand will lay hold on all your enemies; your right hand will seize your foes. ⁹When you appear for battle, you will burn them up as in a blazing furnace. The L*ORD *will swallow them up in his wrath, and his fire will consume them. ¹⁰You will destroy their descendants from the earth, their posterity from mankind. ¹¹Though they plot evil against you and devise wicked schemes, they cannot succeed. ¹²You will make them turn their backs when you aim at them with drawn bow.*

*¹³Be exalted in your strength, L*ORD*; we will sing and praise your might.*

Key Observation. God's dependable and loyal love secures the future for God's people.

Understanding the Word. If Psalm 20 gives words for praying for the Lord to give victory to Israel's earthly king, Psalm 21 gives thanks to the Lord for this victory. These two psalms offer a key pattern that must be practiced in our lives of faith: petition and gratitude. As we've seen, we can bring requests of all types to God in the anticipation of God hearing our prayers. Let us also cultivate the practice of celebratory gratitude for the blessings (great and small) that we receive from God.

God gave the king victory over those who threatened God's people and mission to bless the nations. Verses 1–7 focus on expressing thanks to God for this victory. The focus is not on the power or craftiness of the king. The prayer recognized that the king's victory depended solely on God's power and provision. In other words, this is a psalm celebrating God's victory. The king was successful because God is strong. The king was victorious because God granted the victory. The king was alive and well because God sustained him.

This God-centered perspective is vital. In prayer, we give God the glory. Praising God shows our recognition and dependence on God. To make it through the world we need more than our individual and collective gifts, talents, and resources. We may follow godly leaders, but their success turns on their trusting dependence on the Lord. Verse 7 emphasizes the king's *trust* was the basis for his success. The Lord's dependable love and loyalty ensured the king's future.

In the second half of Psalm 21 (vv. 8–13), the pray-er speaks words of commissioning and empowerment over the king. These lines focus on promises for ongoing success. These promises stood on the relationship of deep trust between the king and Lord. The king would succeed because he was the Lord's anointed. Future enemies would already be defeated. Reflect on the power of these promises of victory and protection. The king was free to practice faithfulness and lead God's people because he could act in the knowledge and confidence that God had his back.

There is profound freedom in feeling deep in our being that our future is secure. Psalm 2 opens the Psalter with this promise. As we move through times of lament, challenge, and suffering, we can lose sight of God's guarantee. The Lord secured the future through Jesus' life, death, and resurrection. Jesus is our true King. Jesus triumphed over the grave and defeated all of the forces of wickedness, sin, brokenness, alienation, sadness, sickness, and injustice.

We live our lives now in hopeful anticipation of the full manifestation of God's love in the future kingdom. This puts us in a powerful position. We can live courageously in the present because we know that our *past* is forgiven and that our *future* is secure. This was the privileged position of the king in Psalm 21, but it can be ours today as well.

Verse 13 ends the psalm by reminding us that it is God who has done these great things and whose strength and power will guide us. We are his witnesses.

1. How did the psalmist model how we should pray when we've experienced God's deliverance in our lives or witnessed it working in the life of someone that we care about?

2. Why is it important to recognize our dependence on God?

3. What would you do for God today if you knew that your future was completely secure?

THREE

God Our True King

Psalm 24 ESV *The earth is the LORD's and the fullness thereof, the world and those who dwell therein, ²for he has founded it upon the seas and established it upon the rivers.*

³Who shall ascend the hill of the LORD? And who shall stand in his holy place? ⁴He who has clean hands and a pure heart, who does not lift up his soul to what is false and does not swear deceitfully. ⁵He will receive blessing from the LORD and righteousness from the God of his salvation. ⁶Such is the generation of those who seek him, who seek the face of the God of Jacob.

⁷Lift up your heads, O gates! And be lifted up, O ancient doors, that the King of glory may come in. ⁸Who is this King of glory? The LORD, strong and mighty, the LORD, mighty in battle! ⁹Lift up your heads, O gates! And lift them up, O ancient doors, that the King of glory may come in. ¹⁰Who is this King of glory? The LORD of hosts, he is the King of glory!

Key Observation. As Creator and Sustainer of the universe, God is the *only* true King.

Understanding the Word. Psalm 24 is a powerful declaration of the Lord's kingship. It flows through three movements: verses 1–2 declare God's credentials as Creator, verses 3–6 describe the character of his followers, and verses 7–10 welcome God's arrival by announcing his victory. This psalm was probably originally used in temple services that celebrated the Lord as King of creation. We can read it profitably as a prayer of praise to our Lord and a call to holiness as we seek to reflect his character to the world.

Verses 1–2 identify the Lord as the Creator and ruler of the earth. This is an important declaration in the ancient world. It is the means by which a god demonstrates his superiority over all others. Since the Lord can secure the earth and make it a safe place for life, then this proves that the Lord is truly Lord of all. The opening verses invite us to recognize God as King and to dethrone any "little" kings in our lives that may diminish our capacity to serve and trust the true King.

Verses 3–6 turn to the worshipers who have gathered to celebrate the Lord as King. Verse 3 asks a question of credentials: Who is able to gather in the temple to await the coming victorious Creator and King? Verses 4–6 answer this question by focusing on *character* rather than social status or accomplishment. Verse 4 focuses our attention on our inner motives. The language is "clean [innocent] hands and a pure heart." *Heart* is the intellectual and decision-making center of a person. In other words, God's people are to be whole persons whose inner motivations are in line with the mission and will of God. This proper alignment of our intentions with God's will then flows into our actions that we take with our hands, feet, and mouths. The key to living from a purity of heart is trust. In our world, there are gods screaming out for our devotion and trust: wealth, security, sex, family, and status are a few examples. Those who turn from these little gods to trust fully in Jesus and walk faithfully in following his way will find their way to the gathering of them that await the victorious Lord.

Verses 7–10 narrate the arrival of the victorious King of the world. In each of these verses, God bears the title "the King of glory." This is a statement of God's awesomeness or incomparability. There is no one like the Lord. The King of glory is the Lord Almighty. As Christians, we read this psalm as a celebration of the crucified and risen Lord Jesus. Paul wrote in Philippians 2:10–11, "at the name of Jesus every knee should bow, in heaven and on earth and under the earth, and every tongue acknowledge that Jesus Christ is Lord." The Lord Jesus has secured our future and our world. We give him our worship and adoration as we await his return to usher in the New Creation.

1. How does this psalm describe our foundation for true security?

2. What is the link between character and worship in Psalm 24?

3. What is the basis for worshiping the Lord according to this psalm?

FOUR
Praying with Trust

Psalm 25:1–7 *In you, LORD my God, I put my trust.*

²I trust in you; do not let me be put to shame, nor let my enemies triumph over me. ³No one who hopes in you will ever be put to shame, but shame will come on those who are treacherous without cause.

⁴Show me your ways, LORD, teach me your paths. ⁵Guide me in your truth and teach me, for you are God my Savior, and my hope is in you all day long. ⁶Remember, LORD, your great mercy and love, for they are from of old. ⁷Do not remember the sins of my youth and my rebellious ways; according to your love remember me, for you, LORD, are good.

Key Observation. God listens to prayers rooted in a posture of deep trust and dependence.

Understanding the Word. Psalm 25 is a lament grounded in deep trust. The psalmist prayed to the Lord for forgiveness of sin and protection from enemies. This psalm teaches us to pray in trying times and invites us to receive and act on the Lord's instruction to forge a godly character.

Psalm 25 uses an acrostic design. This means that in the original Hebrew each successive verse begins with the next letter in the Hebrew alphabet. This gives the psalm a unity and completeness. Verse 1 begins with the letter *aleph* (the first letter in the Hebrew alphabet) and verse 21 with the letter *tav* (the last letter in the Hebrew alphabet). Verse 22 stands outside of the acrostic design and brings the psalm to a conclusion with a final plea for help.

In verses 1–2, the psalmist twice declared his trust in the Lord. He addressed the Lord as "my God." He recognized his dependence on the Lord. This is the proper posture by which to approach the King of glory (see Psalm 24). The psalmist then petitioned the Lord to keep him from shame and from the triumphs of his enemies. Verse 3 validates the psalmist's faith in the form of an affirmation that those who hope in the Lord will be spared shame at the hands of their enemies. The Lord will instead shame those who are intent on acting wickedly.

The psalmist recognized his dependence on God, and in verses 4–7 asked for the Lord's instruction so that he could walk faithfully through the world.

Thus far, we've read psalms in which there is a clear line between the righteous and the wicked. The psalmist in Psalm 25 included himself with the righteous, but demonstrates a key trait for God's people to nurture: a teachable spirit mixed with a desire for growth.

In verses 4–5a, the psalmist prayed, "Show me your ways." This was a prayer for the Lord to cause the psalmist to *know* the Lord's ways or paths. The assumption is that life is a journey and guidance is necessary. A second assumption is that God is willing and able to *teach*. The psalmist understood that he needed the GPS of God to help him navigate the world.

In verses 5b–7, the psalmist grounded his prayer in his confidence in the Lord's character. In verse 5b, the psalmist declared his loyalty to God. The psalmist was all trusting. The Lord was plan A, B, C, and D. He recognized that the Lord was his God and his Savior.

The psalmist appealed to the core of the Lord's character: his mercy and faithful love (cf. Exodus 34:6–7a). These are the traits that the Lord demonstrated in saving God's people from bondage in Egypt and in revealing to God's people the law on Sinai. The psalmist trusted that God would deal with him in the same way. The psalmist recognized his own need for cleansing and asked God to deal with him out of his love and goodness.

As we seek to grow into the people whom God desires for us to be, let us pray out of dependence and need while opening ourselves to God's cleansing and empowerment.

1. What role did dependence on God play in the psalmist's faith?

2. What are the traits of a person dependent on God?

3. How, specifically, does Psalm 25:1–7 teach us to pray?

FIVE

Praying to a Good God

Psalm 25:8–22 *Good and upright is the LORD; therefore he instructs sinners in his ways. ⁹He guides the humble in what is right and teaches them his way. ¹⁰All the ways of the LORD are loving and faithful toward those who keep the demands* *of his covenant. ¹¹For the sake of your name, LORD, forgive my iniquity, though it is great.*

¹²Who, then, are those who fear the LORD? He will instruct them in the ways they should choose. ¹³They will spend their days in prosperity, and their descendants will inherit the land. ¹⁴The LORD confides in those who fear him; he makes his covenant known to them. ¹⁵My eyes are ever on the LORD, for only he will release my feet from the snare.

¹⁶Turn to me and be gracious to me, for I am lonely and afflicted. ¹⁷Relieve the troubles of my heart and free me from my anguish. ¹⁸Look on my affliction and my distress and take away all my sins. ¹⁹See how numerous are my enemies and how fiercely they hate me!

²⁰Guard my life and rescue me; do not let me be put to shame, for I take refuge in you. ²¹May integrity and uprightness protect me, because my hope, LORD, is in you.

²²Deliver Israel, O God, from all their troubles!

Key Observation. We can pray with confidence to God because God is truly good.

Understanding the Word. In verses 1–7, the psalmist declared his trust and dependence on the Lord and appealed to the Lord's love, mercy, and goodness as the basis for forgiving his sins and delivering him from enemies.

In the remainder of the psalm (vv. 8–22) the psalmist reiterated his need for deliverance and his belief in the Lord's goodness. The psalmist moved back and forth in his prayer between proclaiming the guidance and kindness of God with his petitions for God to act to save him.

Verses 8–11 illustrate this well. In verses 8–10, the psalmist praised the Lord for his instruction and guidance. These flow directly out of God's character. The psalmist described the Lord as good, upright, loving, and faithful. In other words, the Lord embodies the positive traits that we long to experience in our own lives. The psalmist appealed to these core characteristics of the Lord by crying out for forgiveness for his own sense of lostness. Notice the phrase in verse 11, "for the sake of your name, LORD." The psalmist desired forgiveness not only as means of saving his own neck but for the testimony and honor that it would provide for the Lord. The psalmist could again join in the chorus of creation that would testify to the Lord's goodness to those who did not know the Lord.

In verses 12–21, the pattern repeats. The psalmist described God's character and actions (vv. 12–14) and then the psalmist followed with a longer list of petitions (vv. 15–21). Verses 12–14 describe the benefits of being in proper relationship with the Lord ("those who fear the LORD"). God will instruct them and give them prosperity. The assumption is that God's people desire and receive this guidance. Verse 14 mentions "covenant." This likely refers to the Sinai covenant. At Sinai, God offered his people a relationship rooted in grace.

In verses 15–21, the psalmist aligned himself and his hope for a future with the Lord. He saw in God the only means of release from his bondage and affliction. The psalmist struggled internally as a result of his sins, but he also faced serious challenges and danger from numerous enemies all around him. He released all of his hurts and desires to God. This is a key step in prayer. The pray-er relinquishes to God all concerns. Doing this allows God's people to live in the moment and free themselves from the affliction of worry. Verse 21 is a final proclamation of the psalmist's personal trust. The psalmist was direct: "my hope, LORD, is in you." The psalmist did not waffle between options. If there was a way out, it would be through the help of the Lord.

The psalmist concluded Psalm 25 with a general petition for God to act on behalf of his people to deliver them from *all* their troubles. This final verse reminds us that true piety can never be confined to our experiences as individuals. We must be mindful of our neighbor in our prayers too.

1. How does Psalm 25:8–22 teach us the importance of praise, trust, and making requests of God?

2. What aspects of your life do you have a difficult time relinquishing to God in prayer? Do you trust God enough to day to take the next step?

3. What does verse 22 teach us about the relationship between community and our individual prayers?

WEEK SEVEN

GATHERING DISCUSSION OUTLINE

A. Open session in prayer.

B. View video for this week's reading.

C. What general impressions and thoughts do you have after considering the video and reading the daily writings on these Scriptures? What specifically did this week's psalms teach you about faith, life, and prayer? How, specifically, do these psalms understand the basis for true security?

D. Discuss selected questions from the daily readings.

1. **KEY OBSERVATION (PSALM 20):** God's kingdom is secure because of God's protection, not because of human power, weaponry, or tactics.

   DISCUSSION QUESTION: How does this psalm teach us to pray for protection for God's people, the church of Jesus? How challenging is it for us today to adopt the instruction of the psalmist?

2. **KEY OBSERVATION (PSALM 21):** God's dependable and loyal love secures the future for God's people.

   DISCUSSION QUESTION: What would you do for God today if you knew that your future was completely secure?

3. **KEY OBSERVATION (PSALM 24):** As Creator and Sustainer of the universe, God is the *only* true King.

   DISCUSSION QUESTION: How does Psalm 24 describe our foundation for true security?

4. **KEY OBSERVATION (PSALM 25:1–7):** God listens to prayers rooted in a posture of deep trust and dependence.

   DISCUSSION QUESTION: What role does dependence on God play in the psalmist's faith?

5. **KEY OBSERVATION (PSALM 25:8–22):** We can pray with confidence to God because God is truly good.

   DISCUSSION QUESTION: How does Psalm 25:8–22 teach us the importance of praise, trust, and making requests of God? What aspects of your life do you have a difficult time relinquishing to God in prayer?

E. Close session with prayer.

WEEK EIGHT

Psalms 22–23

Our Shepherd of Abundance in All Circumstances

INTRODUCTION

This week we will explore two popular psalms: Psalm 22 and Psalm 23. Each is instantly recognizable by its initial verse. Jesus memorably uttered the opening line of Psalm 22 from the cross: "My God, my God, why have you forsaken me?" Psalm 23 begins, "The LORD is my shepherd. I lack nothing."

That two of the best-known psalms occur back-to-back is no coincidence. As we've seen, there is an inner coherence and structure to the Psalter. Although we can pray each of its prayers individually, there is richness in praying each within its context. Psalm 22 opens with the hopelessness of God-forsakenness. Yet the very next psalm expresses the deepest trust in the Lord's care and a vision of the abundance of life in all circumstances.

Psalm 22 is a psalm of two contrasting halves. In the opening sections (vv. 1–21), the reader encounters a poignant lament by an individual who was desperate for deliverance. The psalmist offered a cycle of lament followed by praise that recurs three times (vv. 1–2, 3–5; vv. 6–8, 9–11; vv. 12–18, 19–21). Verses 19–21 serve as a pivotal section. In these verses, the psalmist turned from confessing and praising God as he had in verses 3–5 and 9–11 to requesting deliverance from God. Psalm 22 shifts at this point and morphs into a thanksgiving for deliverance. This is a complete reversal in tone. If verses 1–21 describe a person in deep despair, we will see that verses 22–31 celebrate God's deliverance.

Psalm 23 follows the passionate prayer of Psalm 22 with a beautiful depiction of the bounty of abundance found in the Lord by those who trust him.

Psalm 23 reflects richly on life when each of us rests moment by moment in the reality that God is truly *our* shepherd.

Psalm 23 paints a portrait of security, tranquility, and abundance. Yet it is a psalm that recognizes the challenges of life in the present. The game changer, however, is this: whether we are in the valley or on the mountain, God is with us and guides us on the pathways of life. But it is even better. This psalm envisions a life of blessedness.

Psalm 23 is an apt word of testimony following the agony and ecstasy of the psalmist's journey of faith described in Psalm 22. Recognizing this, we will read these texts in unison this week.

ONE

Feeling Forsaken

Psalm 22:1–11 *My God, my God, why have you forsaken me? Why are you so far from saving me, so far from my cries of anguish?* ²*My God, I cry out by day, but you do not answer, by night, but I find no rest.*

³*Yet you are enthroned as the Holy One; you are the one Israel praises.* ⁴*In you our ancestors put their trust; they trusted and you delivered them.* ⁵*To you they cried out and were saved; in you they trusted and were not put to shame.*

⁶*But I am a worm and not a man, scorned by everyone, despised by the people.* ⁷*All who see me mock me; they hurl insults, shaking their heads.* ⁸*"He trusts in the* LORD*," they say, "let the* LORD *rescue him. Let him deliver him, since he delights in him."*

⁹*Yet you brought me out of the womb; you made me trust in you, even at my mother's breast.* ¹⁰*From birth I was cast on you; from my mother's womb you have been my God.*

¹¹*Do not be far from me, for trouble is near and there is no one to help.*

Key Observation. Jesus truly identifies with us *in* our suffering and will lift us up to victory *in the midst of our pain.*

Understanding the Word. Psalm 22 begins in desperation: "My God, my God, why have you forsaken me?" We likely know these words best because Jesus uttered them from the cross (see Matthew 27:46 and Mark 15:34).

Christ's followers have long read Psalm 22 in light of Jesus' death because the Gospels invite us to do this. The description of the suffering of the psalmist in Psalm 22 connects powerfully and specifically with the abuse and trauma that Jesus experienced during his crucifixion.

As we read and study Psalm 22, it is important to see the connections between both Jesus' death (vv. 1–21) and resurrection (vv. 22–31). But it is also crucial for us to hear Psalm 22 as a psalm that reflects deeply on suffering and thanksgiving as we may experience it. In other words, Psalm 22 does point to Jesus' death and resurrection, but Jesus chose to speak the words of Psalm 22 because he wanted each of us to understand, know, and feel deep inside of our beings that God truly identifies with us in *our* suffering and will lift us up to victory *in the midst of our pain.* This is good news.

Psalm 22:1–2 are the words of a person desperate to hear from God. We do not know the precise specifics of the psalmist's plight, but he was in a difficult setting and he felt far from God. It is a time when prayers seem to go unanswered and sleep is nowhere to be found despite our weariness. This is lament to the core. When Jesus spoke these words, he did not literally mean that God had left him. Rather he identified with human suffering and the feeling in the moment of utter abandonment. When we pray to God out of our desperation, remember that Jesus understands precisely how it feels to be in such a condition.

Remember also that extreme despair is no indication of our faith commitments. Notice in verses 1–11 that the psalmist alternated between desperate lament (vv. 1–2 and 6–8) and passionate praise (vv. 3–5 and 9–11). Some of the most beautiful lyrics of worship are here. Verses 3–5 recognize God's power and prestige as the "Holy One." God can be trusted and generations of believers have testified to this truth. They prayed to the Lord and found deliverance. This *faith* is the grounds for the psalmist's prayer to God. The psalmist wanted to experience the same deliverance that others had witnessed.

But at that time, the psalmist was in crisis. Verses 6–8 return us to the psalmist's reality. These words remind us of the forsakenness of Jesus on the cross and mocking of the crowds as he died. The mocking includes cynical remarks about the futility of the sufferer's faith.

Yet the psalmist again returned to praise in verses 9–11. The praise was then more personal. The psalmist remembered God's previous work in his own life. God had guided him from birth. This was reason for hope in the suffering. In verse 11, the psalmist affirmed his belief that only God could help him.

1. Have there been times in your life that you identified with the psalmist's sense of forsakenness?

2. What is the relationship between prayers of help and our words of praise?

3. How does Jesus' identification with our suffering shape how we understand and experience times of trial?

TWO

Desperate for Deliverance

Psalm 22:12–21 *Many bulls surround me; strong bulls of Bashan encircle me. [13]Roaring lions that tear their prey open their mouths wide against me. [14]I am poured out like water, and all my bones are out of joint. My heart has turned to wax; it has melted within me. [15]My mouth is dried up like a potsherd, and my tongue sticks to the roof of my mouth; you lay me in the dust of death.*

[16]Dogs surround me, a pack of villains encircles me; they pierce my hands and my feet. [17]All my bones are on display; people stare and gloat over me. [18]They divide my clothes among them and cast lots for my garment.

[19]But you, LORD, do not be far from me. You are my strength; come quickly to help me. [20]Deliver me from the sword, my precious life from the power of the dogs. [21]Rescue me from the mouth of the lions; save me from the horns of the wild oxen.

Key Observation. Our faith can sustain us through the darkest moments of life.

Understanding the Word. The plight of the psalmist reached its pinnacle in verses 12–18, but his faith was never more steady than in verses 19–21.

The intensity of the psalmist's lament boiled in these verses. There appeared to be no way out for the psalmist. He metaphorically viewed his enemies as wild and ravenous beasts seeking his life (vv. 12–13). Close your eyes and picture yourself surrounded by any of the following: a herd of angry bulls, a pride of hungry lions, or a pack of wild dogs. Terrifying. This is how the psalmist felt. His body responded physically to the terror and pain (vv. 14–15).

Verses 12–18 connect directly with Jesus' last hours on the cross. He cried out in thirst, opponents surrounded him, and the soldiers responsible for his execution gambled for his clothing.

These verses are meant to sound extreme because suffering is devastating and shocking. We've all experienced it in some form. Whether it's the loss of a loved one, the suffering caused by illness (our own or of a loved one), the loneliness and grief of a broken relationship or marriage, or the aftermath of some other trauma, the words of Psalm 22 give us vocabulary and phrases and serve to model prayer for moments of authentic desperation. Jesus looked to this psalm. So can we.

If verses 12–18 function as the psalmist's words as he reached the bottom of the pit, it is profound to remember and recognize that God is still present. This is one of the most vital resources for the faithful. We may reach the end of our rope, exhaust all of our resources, and have no one on earth to help us, but our future is not dependent on any part of creation. The psalmist continued to place hope in God, and in verses 19–21 offered a final impassioned cry and prayer for help. Read the psalmist's words in these verses again. Note how they connect with his description of his plight.

When we pray to God, we do not have to sugarcoat our words. The promise of the gospel is that God already knows our needs (see Matthew 6:8). So why hide our true feelings and deepest desires? Enemies who seem like famished beasts surrounded the psalmist. So what did he pray for? The psalmist asked specifically for deliverance and rescue from dogs, lions, and wild oxen. Notice that these are in the reverse sequence of their appearance in vv. 12–18 where the order was bulls, lions, and dogs. In other words, the psalmist asked specifically, precisely, and boldly for exactly what he most desperately needed.

The psalmist prayed for God's presence and help (v. 19). This is the key to prayer. The psalmist recognized that God was present, able, willing, and powerful enough to save. Sometimes we mistakenly believe that it is the amount of our faith that activates God's actions. It's not. Faith is only as powerful as its object. Our God is able to hear our prayers and bring deliverance. Jesus prayed Psalm 22. This did not alleviate his suffering immediately, but we know that resurrection occurred on the other side of suffering and death. The psalmist in

Psalm 22 experienced deliverance and answer to his prayers. He will tell us this story in the concluding verses of the psalm (vv. 22–31).

1. How do verses 12–21 teach us to pray in the midst of our suffering?

2. What role does faith play in our prayers for help?

3. How do these verses remind us of Jesus' suffering on the cross?

THREE

Celebrating Salvation

Psalm 22:22–31 ESV *I will tell of your name to my brothers; in the midst of the congregation I will praise you:* ²³*You who fear the LORD, praise him! All you offspring of Jacob, glorify him, and stand in awe of him, all you offspring of Israel!* ²⁴*For he has not despised or abhorred the affliction of the afflicted, and he has not hidden his face from him, but has heard, when he cried to him.*

²⁵*From you comes my praise in the great congregation; my vows I will perform before those who fear him.* ²⁶*The afflicted shall eat and be satisfied; those who seek him shall praise the LORD! May your hearts live forever!*

²⁷*All the ends of the earth shall remember and turn to the LORD, and all the families of the nations shall worship before you.* ²⁸*For kingship belongs to the LORD, and he rules over the nations.*

²⁹*All the prosperous of the earth eat and worship; before him shall bow all who go down to the dust, even the one who could not keep himself alive.* ³⁰*Posterity shall serve him; it shall be told of the Lord to the coming generation;* ³¹*they shall come and proclaim his righteousness to a people yet unborn, that he has done it.*

Key Observation. God's raising of Jesus from the dead secures our future.

Understanding the Word. Poignant lament becomes a testimony of thanksgiving when God answers our prayer. For the psalmist of Psalm 22, lament turned to thanksgiving and praise at verse 22. The sorrow of the opening verse, "My God, my God, why have you forsaken me?" morphs into an audacious and free testimony about the power of the Lord to work salvation even in the most hopeless situation.

How do we respond to God's saving work in our lives? With gratitude and public witness. The psalmist knew that God has saved him and made certain that God got the credit (v. 22).

Notice that the psalmist's testimony included inviting the community to participate in the celebration (v. 23). This is an important reminder that even psalms that sound individualistic are intended to be shared in community. Following Jesus is not a solitary enterprise. We must always stay connected to our community in times of plenty and in times of want. The psalmist experienced isolation in verses 1–21. Verses 22–31 model the importance of communal celebration.

Verses 24–25 remind us of the psalmist's previous plight and summarizes his newfound testimony. He had experienced isolation and trauma. He had felt rejected by God. Yet the psalmist declared the truth: *God remained with him.* This is deep truth for us. We may feel rejected and alone, but God abides with us. Jesus, who knows suffering and pain, is our High Priest (see Hebrews 4:14–16) and extends grace to us in our times of need. God hears our cries and prayers, even our most desperate ones. Moreover, God acts and provides the pray-er with a testimony to share (v. 25).

The deliverance of the psalmist is good news for the world. Verses 26–29 turn to the implications of the psalmist's experience of salvation for others. God doesn't just save "me"; God is willing, ready, and able to deliver others. The "others" include the poor, all who seek the Lord, and even people from the surrounding nations who turn to the Lord. This reminds us of God's mission. God's people exist as conduits of God's grace for the world. This means that our testimony serves not only to encourage other believers but as a word about God's kingdom to those who do not yet follow Jesus. Verses 26–29 are inclusive of all: from the prosperous to needy. Verse 29 even hints at persons who have already passed on. The point is this: *God's grace, love, and blessings are available to all who turn to him.* The psalmist experienced this personally and shared this good news with his community and the world.

Verses 30–31 conclude the psalm by emphasizing God's work in bringing deliverance and salvation. God's acts of grace will carry on and future generations will here of it. The final verdict on human history is this: "He has done it."

Jesus spoke Psalm 22:1 on the cross. Yet Jesus' death was not the end; God raised Jesus from the dead to secure our future. He has done it indeed. Amen.

1. What does Psalm 22:22–31 teach us about gratitude and giving thanks for God's victory?

2. How can we incorporate thanksgiving into our personal lives and into our worship experiences?

3. How does giving thanks advance God's mission in the world?

FOUR

My Shepherd

Psalm 23:1 *The LORD is my shepherd, I lack nothing.*

Key Observation. Our Lord is a capable and faithful Shepherd who looks out for the best interests of the flock.

Understanding the Word. Following the passionate lament and thanksgiving of Psalm 22, Psalm 23 serves as a declaration of deep trust in the Lord. Psalm 23 is written from a first-person individual perspective. It serves as a prayer or meditation on one's own faith in the Lord's provision. Is there any better response to the reality of God's presence in any circumstance than reflecting on the depths of our own trust in his faithfulness?

Verse 1 begins memorably with the psalmist reflecting on his relationship with God. The psalmist chose the words carefully and they are ripe with meaning: "*The LORD is my shepherd.*" The psalmist knew God personally and relationally. The psalmist prayed *my* Shepherd and not *our* Shepherd, *his* Shepherd, *her* Shepherd, *your* Shepherd, or *their* Shepherd. Don't rush past this observation. Trust manifests in the individual. Psalm 23 invites us to pray and proclaim our own individual faith in the Lord. Martin Luther once wrote, "Every man must do two things alone; he must do his own believing and his own dying." What does this mean if you are struggling in your faith? Again the Psalter provides words for us to offer to God in times of bounty and scarcity, on days of unshakeable faith and on days when we are closer to the words of

101

the father out of whose son Jesus had cast a demon, "I do believe; help me overcome my unbelief" (Mark 9:24). The faith expressed in Psalm 23 can even inspire us in times when we find ourselves barely able to pray at all—when we are teetering on unbelief. The power of Psalm 23 is its ability to sustain us even in the darkest hours.

The key is not the strength of *my* faith but its object. Psalm 23 directs our faith onto the Lord. In Psalm 23, the Lord is imaged as *Shepherd*. What do shepherds do? They abide with, take care of, protect, and guide a flock of sheep. The sheep can live their lives safe from all harm because of the skill, power, care, compassion, and commitment of the shepherd. This is the metaphor that the psalmist offered us for contemplation as we pray. The psalmist assumed that God is a capable and faithful Shepherd who looks out for the best interests of the flock. In John 10:11, Jesus exclaimed, "I am the good shepherd. The good shepherd lays down his life for the sheep."

What flows from an intimate trust in the care of the Lord as *my* Shepherd? It is the realization of my own lack of need. If God is truly my Shepherd, I am in need of nothing. The same God who invites us to request, "Give us today our daily bread" (Matt. 6:11) can be trusted with all aspects and areas of life: financial, relational, physical, and spiritual. Praying "I lack nothing" (Ps. 23:1) also puts me in a position of generosity. As my needs are met, I can look outward to the needs of those around me.

1. How does Psalm 23 challenge you to think about your needs and sense of lack in your life?

2. What does it mean for you to pray, "The Lord is *my* Shepherd"?

3. What does the imagery of "shepherd" tell us about God?

FIVE

Abundance and Security

Psalm 23:2–6 *He makes me lie down in green pastures, he leads me beside quiet waters, ³he refreshes my soul. He guides me along the right paths for his name's sake. ⁴Even though I walk through the darkest valley, I will fear no evil, for you are with me; your rod and your staff, they comfort me.*

⁵You prepare a table before me in the presence of my enemies. You anoint my head with oil; my cup overflows. ⁶Surely your goodness and love will follow me all the days of my life, and I will dwell in the house of the LORD forever.

Key Observation. God promises to guide us through hardship and darkness to a future of abundance.

Understanding the Word. Psalm 23 continues with reflection on the meaning of the Lord serving as the Good Shepherd of our lives. Verses 2–6 offer specific ways in which the Lord serves as the Shepherd that each of us longs to address as *my* Shepherd.

Verses 2–3 build immediately on the declaration of Psalm 23:1 with beautiful imagery of tranquility and peace. All is well in the life of the sheep. The Good Shepherd provides all that the flock requires and actively guides each sheep down the paths of righteousness. These verses ground the pray-er in abundance before reflecting on the challenges of life.

In verse three, we learn that the Lord restores the soul of the psalmist. It is the Hebrew word *nephesh* that is translated "soul" here. Nephesh is used in a similar fashion in the Great Commandment: Love the LORD your God with all your heart and with all your soul and with all your strength" (Deut. 6:5). *Soul* is the traditional English translation and is a good one provided that we do not limit its meaning to the *spiritual* aspect of ourselves apart from the body. In the Old Testament usage, the soul is the totality of our being. We don't have a soul; we are a soul. The soul, or nephesh, is our enlivened body. This is important. The Shepherd in Psalm 23 does not merely restore some spiritual part of us; the Lord restores *all* of us. The abundance that God offers his people includes the physical and the spiritual.

In verse 4, the tone and the perspective of the psalm changes. Just in case we have been misreading the good news of Psalm 23, it gets better. The Good Shepherd is no fair-weather friend. The Lord is the kind of Shepherd who is all in for his flock even in the toughest times in life. *Darkest valley* is traditionally translated "shadow of death." In other words, the Lord is present and guiding each member of his flock in all circumstances, even those that put us in danger of death itself. Verse 4 helps us to understand the right paths of verse 3 more clearly. The pathways of life will likely include both times of joy and times of sorrowful trouble. Yet, God remains steadfast in faithfully guiding us through.

The psalmist was so overwhelmed by the realization of God's presence even in the darkest valley that the prayer shifts from third-person language *about* God to second-person language *to* God. This is prayer at its best. Psalm 23 shifts from a song of trust *about* God to a prayer of faith *to* God. God was no mere object in the psalmist's life. God was subject and in relationship with the psalmist. What does this mean? It means that we practice our faith by talking with God rather than merely talking or thinking about God.

God was with the psalmist and brought comfort to him at the point of deepest need. The Shepherd used his rod and staff not as a weapon to punish the psalmist but to guide and comfort.

Verses 5–6 shifts the prayer to its climactic end. The imagery is of a victory feast. The fields, pathways, and valleys have morphed into a well-set table. Abundance had triumphed. All of the threats and enemies stood defeated. God prepared and offered a bountiful buffet for the psalmist with former enemies and the dark moments of life were in the background watching.

The message is clear. Trusting God leads to security and abundance. Hardship and darkness will not have the final say. In fact, the pray-er ends with a powerful affirmation of God's goodness and love in the full confidence that he will abide in God's presence forever (v. 6).

1. How would you live your life differently if you truly believed that an abundant and good future awaited you?

2. Why do you think that the compiler of the psalms placed Psalm 23 directly after Psalm 22?

3. Which of these two psalms do you find most helpful at this stage of your life?

WEEK EIGHT

GATHERING DISCUSSION OUTLINE

A. Open session in prayer.

B. View video for this week's reading.

C. What general impressions and thoughts do you have after considering the video and reading the daily writings on these Scriptures? What specifically did this week's psalms teach you about faith, life, and prayer? What did you learn by reading Psalms 22 and 23 in light of one another this week?

D. Discuss selected questions from the daily readings.

1. **KEY OBSERVATION (PSALM 22:1–11):** Jesus truly identifies with us *in* our suffering and will lift us up to victory *in the midst of our pain.*

DISCUSSION QUESTION: How does Jesus' identification with our suffering shape how we understand and experience times of trial?

2. **KEY OBSERVATION (PSALM 22:12–21):** Our faith can sustain us through the darkest moments of life.

DISCUSSION QUESTION: How do verses 12–21 teach us to pray in the midst of our suffering?

3. **KEY OBSERVATION (PSALM 22:22–31):** God's raising of Jesus from the dead secures our future.

DISCUSSION QUESTION: What does Psalm 22:22–31 teach us about gratitude and giving thanks for God's victory?

4. **KEY OBSERVATION (PSALM 23:1):** Our Lord is a capable and faithful Shepherd who looks out for the best interests of the flock.

   DISCUSSION QUESTION: What does it mean for you to pray, "The Lord is *my* shepherd"? What does the imagery of a shepherd tell us about God?

5. **KEY OBSERVATION (PSALM 23:2–6):** God promises to guide us through hardship and darkness to a future of abundance.

   DISCUSSION QUESTION: How would you live your life differently if you truly believed that an abundant and good future awaited you?

E. Close session with prayer.

WEEK NINE

Psalms 26–29

Lament and Praise

INTRODUCTION

This week we will study three more laments (Psalms 26–28) and a hymn of praise (Psalm 29). This interplay of lament with the other genres continues the pattern that we've seen from Psalm 3 forward.

In our present context, recall our studies from the previous weeks. Psalms 3–17 were mostly laments. This is important because it introduced the cry for help as a core prayer for God's people as they seek to live as his missional people in the world. As we seek to live faithfully as followers of Jesus, we will encounter times of want and deep need. God does not expect us to put on a happy face and live with whatever pain or turmoil may come. Instead, these psalms teach us to pray in all circumstances. One of the core issues that they attempt to resolve for us is the issue of security. As believers, when we experience the disorienting effects of pain in our lives, we turn to our faith for strength. The laments show us how to pray in faith for deliverance. But faith is only as good as its object.

Psalms 18–24 remind us of the security that we have in the Lord as the foundation for faithful living. These psalms include royal psalms celebrating the Messiah as God's earthly agent of salvation (18 and 20), a Torah psalm rooting us in Scripture (19), thanksgiving psalms showing us how to give thanks for God's salvation (21–22), a psalm of trust (23), and a psalm celebrating the Lord as King (24). These psalms serve as markers on our journey. Psalms 1–2 establish the initial foundation of the Torah and God's reign. Psalms 18–24 reaffirm these core values and recharge our souls as we continue our journey to God's good future as portrayed by Psalms 146–150.

Psalms 25–28 return to lament (remember that we studied Psalm 25 two weeks ago). The implied message of the interplay of the genres is that following Jesus is not an immunization from suffering. We are *secure* in the Lord so we can live boldly and courageously, but we must not be surprised when trouble comes. When it does, we have resources in the Psalms to teach us to pray.

Psalm 29 is another powerful orienting psalm. It praises and celebrates the power of the Lord as King. It uses powerful metaphors drawn from creation to model praise of our true King and source for security in the world.

ONE

Facing Trouble

Psalm 26 ESV *Vindicate me, O LORD, for I have walked in my integrity, and I have trusted in the LORD without wavering. ²Prove me, O LORD, and try me; test my heart and my mind. ³For your steadfast love is before my eyes, and I walk in your faithfulness.*

⁴I do not sit with men of falsehood, nor do I consort with hypocrites. ⁵I hate the assembly of evildoers, and I will not sit with the wicked. ⁶I wash my hands in innocence and go around your altar, O LORD, ⁷proclaiming thanksgiving aloud, and telling all your wondrous deeds.

⁸O LORD, I love the habitation of your house and the place where your glory dwells. ⁹Do not sweep my soul away with sinners, nor my life with bloodthirsty men, ¹⁰in whose hands are evil devices, and whose right hands are full of bribes.

¹¹But as for me, I shall walk in my integrity; redeem me, and be gracious to me. ¹²My foot stands on level ground; in the great assembly I will bless the LORD.

Key Observation. When trouble comes, God's people respond with faithful living and put their hope in God.

Understanding the Word. Psalm 26 is a profound affirmation of personal integrity. Psalm 1 proclaims the "happy" life for those who follow the instruction of the Lord and reject the ways of the world. The psalmist in Psalm 26 had followed this plan perfectly. But there is a problem. Instead of flourishing "like a tree planted by streams of water" (Ps. 1:3), the psalmist was facing serious opposition and feared separation from the God whom he loved. His words can help us to pray when we encounter the silence of God when we need him the most. How do we pray when it seems as though our faithfulness has been in vain?

Psalm 26 contains three movements. In verses 1–3, the psalmist opened with his initial plea for help. In verses 4–8, he proclaimed his faithfulness in following the ways of the Lord. In verses 9–12, he prayed that the Lord would vindicate him.

The psalmist needed a word from the Lord (vv. 1–3). He had done all of the right things. He trusted in the Lord alone. His life was marked by a devotion and grounding in the love and faithfulness of the Lord. Yet there was a problem. He was under assault and needed the Lord to act to save him. But at the moment of that prayer, he did not yet have an answer.

In verses 4–8, the psalmist vigorously described his way of life. In his interactions with the world, he did not associate with the wicked (vv. 4–5). He epitomized the avoidance of evil influences prescribed by Psalm 1:1. Moreover, he actively embodied positive traits that allowed him to reflect God's character in his dealings with the world (vv. 6–8). This is an important emphasis. It is one thing to *avoid* evil or to be *against* something; it is another thing altogether to be *constructive* and be *for* something. In this case, the psalmist was for the ways of the Lord. His life pointed to God. His mode of conduct served as a witness to the Lord. In particular, the psalmist emphasized his practice of worship. The psalmist acted justly in his dealings with others (v. 6a). Then while present in worship, he praised God and told others of God's wonderful deeds of salvation (v. 7). Worship was central to the psalmist, and the psalmist affirmed his love and desire to be near the Lord in the worship at the temple (v. 8).

The psalmist closed his prayer by restating his need for God to act (vv. 9–12). The psalmist desired to continue living for God in the world so he pled for his life lest he end up in the same lot as the wicked. The psalmist could not conceive of this as he had lived a holy life. He trusted God to deliver him. The final verse affirms the psalmist's intention to stand firm in his faith and to praise the Lord in anticipation of salvation.

1. What was the nature of the psalmist's complaint to God?

2. Why do you think that God appears to be silent at times in our life when we most desire his help?

3. What role does our faithfulness play in prayer?

TWO

Waiting for the Lord

Psalm 27 *The Lord is my light and my salvation—whom shall I fear? The Lord is the stronghold of my life—of whom shall I be afraid?*

²When the wicked advance against me to devour me, it is my enemies and my foes who will stumble and fall. ³Though an army besiege me, my heart will not fear; though war break out against me, even then I will be confident.

⁴One thing I ask from the Lord, this only do I seek: that I may dwell in the house of the Lord all the days of my life, to gaze on the beauty of the Lord and to seek him in his temple. ⁵For in the day of trouble he will keep me safe in his dwelling; he will hide me in the shelter of his sacred tent and set me high upon a rock.

⁶Then my head will be exalted above the enemies who surround me; at his sacred tent I will sacrifice with shouts of joy; I will sing and make music to the Lord.

⁷Hear my voice when I call, Lord; be merciful to me and answer me. ⁸My heart says of you, "Seek his face!" Your face, Lord, I will seek. ⁹Do not hide your face from me, do not turn your servant away in anger; you have been my helper. Do not reject me or forsake me, God my Savior. ¹⁰Though my father and mother forsake me, the Lord will receive me. ¹¹Teach me your way, Lord; lead me in a straight path because of my oppressors. ¹²Do not turn me over to the desire of my foes, for false witnesses rise up against me, spouting malicious accusations.

¹³I remain confident of this: I will see the goodness of the Lord in the land of the living. ¹⁴Wait for the Lord; be strong and take heart and wait for the Lord.

Key Observation. During times of crisis, God's people turn away from fear and wait expectantly for God to act.

Understanding the Word. Psalm 27 combines a deep devotion and trust in the Lord with a lament for deliverance from enemies. The language of Psalm 27 is rich and offers us memorable lines to embolden us in our faith as we follow the Lord into the world to embody love for God and love for neighbor.

Psalm 27 opens with a confident declaration of security. Verse 1 contains two rhetorical questions. Since the Lord was the psalmist's life, salvation, and stronghold, whom should the psalmist have feared? The obvious answer was no one. Yet in verses 2–3, the psalmist gave us a hint that there was a potential agent of fear in his life: enemies seeking to trouble him. Psalm 27 captures the reality and tension behind our prayers. We trust the Lord and have confidence in his ways. Yet when we face times of trouble, we still verbalize our fears. The dynamic of prayer allows us to put our faith and hope into words in anticipation of God's answer.

In the middle section of Psalm 27 (vv. 4–6), the psalmist described the security that he found in fellowship and communion with the Lord. This relationship centered on worship in the temple. The psalmist desired deliverance because he had devoted his life to the adoration of God and the nurturing of a relationship with him. The psalmist wanted to be in close proximity to the Lord. This did not mean that the Lord only lived in the temple, but rather it emphasized the symbolic significance of the temple as a place for intentional service and praise. It was the choice location for seeking after the Lord. It was a place of refuge. The psalmist believed that if he could arrive at the temple, he would be secure and experience deliverance (vv. 5–6).

In verses 7–13, the psalmist articulated in detail his pleadings. As we've seen in other laments, the psalmist mixed in statements of his own devotion and faith. In these verses, the psalmist needed an answer (vv. 7, 9, and 12) from the Lord. False witnesses and enemies assailed him. The psalmist pursued God (v. 8) and requested that God shape and form him. He was steadfast in his confidence of a good ending. Even if his parents turned him away, the Lord would still welcome him (v. 10). Likewise he believed that God would demonstrate his goodness and spare his life.

Psalm 27 ends with the psalmist exhorting himself to stand firm and wait for the Lord. He twice reminded himself to *wait*. This is a vital word. Part of the life of faith is surrendering our agendas and time frames and simply trusting God's timing.

1. Describe the tension between the psalmist's faith and his need to ask the Lord for help. What does this tension teach us about the role of prayer?

2. How does worship serve to center you in your walk with God?

3. What aspect of the psalmist's prayer most meaningfully speaks to you? Why?

THREE

Security for All God's People

Psalm 28 *To you, Lord, I call; you are my Rock, do not turn a deaf ear to me. For if you remain silent, I will be like those who go down to the pit. ²Hear my cry for mercy as I call to you for help, as I lift up my hands toward your Most Holy Place.*

³Do not drag me away with the wicked, with those who do evil, who speak cordially with their neighbors but harbor malice in their hearts. ⁴Repay them for their deeds and for their evil work; repay them for what their hands have done and bring back on them what they deserve.

⁵Because they have no regard for the deeds of the Lord and what his hands have done, he will tear them down and never build them up again.

⁶Praise be to the Lord, for he has heard my cry for mercy. ⁷The Lord is my strength and my shield; my heart trusts in him, and he helps me. My heart leaps for joy, and with my song I praise him.

⁸The Lord is the strength of his people, a fortress of salvation for his anointed one. ⁹Save your people and bless your inheritance; be their shepherd and carry them forever.

Key Observation. God provides security for *all* God's people.

Understanding the Word. The language of the Psalms is memorable and important. It provides us with words, metaphors, and images to heighten our connection with God. The language serves to make concrete our ideas and conceptions of who God is and how God works.

Psalm 28 deploys two marvelous images for the Lord at its beginning and end. The psalmist opened his prayer by addressing God as "my Rock" (v. 1). He closed Psalm 28 by asking the Lord to be the "shepherd" of his people (v. 9). Both of these metaphors are ways of describing God as one who is able to *protect* and provide *security* for God's people. This was precisely what the psalmist longed for. Psalm 28 is a lament for protection and deliverance from enemies who are afflicting the pray-er.

The psalmist opened with a plea to the Lord, his Rock, to hear his prayer (v. 1). The psalmist recognized that the Lord is the basis for security. Hence the psalmist addressed the Lord as "my Rock," but in the moment, the psalmist was experiencing *silence* rather than *security*.

The psalmist expanded his pleading in verses 2–4. He was crying out for mercy and prayed toward the temple ("your Most Holy Place"). The last few psalms have referenced the temple. It was a focal point for the religious experience of God's people of Israel. It was a visible reminder of God's presence. As Christians, we don't pray toward a place; we pray through a person: Jesus the Messiah. Jesus embodies the "God with us" presence that the temple represented in the Old Testament. The psalmist pled for God to not include him in the company of the wicked who acted with evil and out of malice (v. 3). He asked God to thwart their evil ways by turning their actions back on them (v. 4).

In verses 5–8, the psalmist shifted to a section of confident praise. He was certain that God would indeed thwart the actions of the wicked so that they would be unable to afflict others (v. 5). Verse 6 anticipates the psalmist's own salvation and gives God praise for hearing his cry. In verse 7, the psalmist deployed another metaphor of security by calling the Lord "my strength and shield." This secure bond formed the basis for the psalmist's deep trust and served as the cause for the psalmist's joy and praise. Verse 8 makes a subtle shift in the praise. The psalmist moved from praising God for the *personal* benefits that he experienced to praising God as the agent of security for *all* God's people and for the Messiah. As we've seen in previous psalms, personal lament needs to broaden to corporate prayer. We may pray for our own needs, but the Psalms model a piety that also includes others in our prayers.

Thus, Psalm 28 ends with a general prayer for the Lord to bring salvation and blessing to God's people as a whole and serve as their Shepherd.

1. What images or metaphors for God do you find most meaningful in this psalm? What other images have captured your imagination from our study of other psalms?

2. How do the images in Psalm 28 communicate the security that we find in the Lord?

3. How does Psalm 28 teach us to pray for security?

FOUR
Praise and God's Greatness

Psalm 29 *Ascribe to the L<small>ORD</small>, you heavenly beings, ascribe to the L<small>ORD</small> glory and strength. ²Ascribe to the L<small>ORD</small> the glory due his name; worship the L<small>ORD</small> in the splendor of his holiness.*

³The voice of the L<small>ORD</small> is over the waters; the God of glory thunders, the L<small>ORD</small> thunders over the mighty waters. ⁴The voice of the L<small>ORD</small> is powerful; the voice of the L<small>ORD</small> is majestic. ⁵The voice of the L<small>ORD</small> breaks the cedars; the L<small>ORD</small> breaks in pieces the cedars of Lebanon. ⁶He makes Lebanon leap like a calf, Sirion like a young wild ox. ⁷The voice of the L<small>ORD</small> strikes with flashes of lightning. ⁸The voice of the L<small>ORD</small> shakes the desert; the L<small>ORD</small> shakes the Desert of Kadesh. ⁹The voice of the L<small>ORD</small> twists the oaks and strips the forests bare. And in his temple all cry, "Glory!"

¹⁰The L<small>ORD</small> sits enthroned over the flood; the L<small>ORD</small> is enthroned as King forever. ¹¹The L<small>ORD</small> gives strength to his people; the L<small>ORD</small> blesses his people with peace.

Key Observation. Praise orients us to the power, greatness, and prestige of the Lord.

Understanding the Word. Psalm 29 is a hymn of praise that serves to declare the eternal kingship of the Lord. This is a psalm of orientation that reminds us of the power, grandeur, and prestige of God. It uses imagery drawn from its ancient Near Eastern context. It uses the imagery of creation and a thunderstorm. This language evoked feelings of awe for its original readers because it touched on core elements of ancient Near Eastern religious thought. We need to read between the lines to hear its rich message in our twenty-first-century world.

In Israel's day, all nations worshiped and served different gods and goddesses. One of the key ways of demonstrating the power of a god or goddess was through stories of the gods controlling and shaping creation. If a god had power over creation, this god could claim to be the true king. Another important element to show a god's strength was the ability to create and sustain life. Rain was central to the well-being of ancient people who depended on rainfall for the growing of food. For the ancient Canaanites, one of the most powerful gods was Baal. If you read through the Old Testament, Baal was one of the foreign deities that God's people often turned to during times of apostasy (e.g., 1 Kings 18:20–40). Baal was the storm god and thus served as a god of fertility. The rain that he sent fertilized the earth and brought forth crops for the ancients.

In Psalm 29, the psalmist drew on language that was similar to the type of images associated with Baal and other similar gods. But there was one major difference. This is a psalm that declares boldly that it is the Lord who is the true King.

As we've been reading through the laments of Book 1 of the Psalter (Psalms 1–41), we've repeatedly read prayers for protection from enemies. As part of these prayers, the psalmists have proclaimed their own integrity, devotion, and commitment to the Lord. We need to read these statements of integrity against the competing religions of the day. If the psalmists had lost their trust in the Lord, it would not mean that they would have become atheists as some do in our day. Instead they would have turned to some other god or goddess—perhaps the god or goddess of the people who were oppressing them.

Psalm 29 works against this by subverting the claims of competing gods. The Scriptures declare that the Lord is incomparable to any other god and, in fact, by the time of Isaiah the prophets declared of the Lord, "Turn to me and be saved, all you ends of the earth; for I am God, and there is no other" (Isa. 45:22). Yet the false worship of idols continued in Israel. Psalm 29 thus uses imagery that others used to worship Baal and shifted the language to make it about the Lord. The psalmist did this to lift up the Lord as our true source of security in the world. He is King. He alone can be trusted with our lives. More on Psalm 29 tomorrow.

1. In our culture, what competes with Jesus for our time, commitment, and trust?

2. Describe the language that Psalm 29 uses to praise the Lord.

3. Can you think of an image or phrase that captures the popular beliefs of our world? How can you repackage it to serve as a message that points to Jesus?

FIVE

Giving the Lord Honor

Psalm 29 *Ascribe to the LORD, you heavenly beings, ascribe to the LORD glory and strength. ²Ascribe to the LORD the glory due his name; worship the LORD in the splendor of his holiness.*

³The voice of the LORD is over the waters; the God of glory thunders, the LORD thunders over the mighty waters. ⁴The voice of the LORD is powerful; the voice of the LORD is majestic. ⁵The voice of the LORD breaks the cedars; the LORD breaks in pieces the cedars of Lebanon. ⁶He makes Lebanon leap like a calf, Sirion like a young wild ox. ⁷The voice of the LORD strikes with flashes of lightning. ⁸The voice of the LORD shakes the desert; the LORD shakes the Desert of Kadesh. ⁹The voice of the LORD twists the oaks and strips the forests bare. And in his temple all cry, "Glory!"

¹⁰The LORD sits enthroned over the flood; the LORD is enthroned as King forever. ¹¹The LORD gives strength to his people; the LORD blesses his people with peace.

Key Observation. Everyone everywhere will grant the Lord the honor and glory due his name.

Understanding the Word. Psalm 29 unfolds in three movements: verses 1–2 are an invitation to the hosts of heaven to worship the Lord, verses 3–9 describe the coming of the Lord in a storm, and verses 10–11 contain God's blessing on his people.

Psalm 29:1–2 exhorts the hosts of heaven to give the Lord the honor due his name and worship him in all of his splendor. Psalm 29 begins not with God's people on the earth but with the beings in the presence of God in his heavenly courtroom. We saw a similar exhortation in Psalm 148:1–2. The scope of the worship implied in Psalm 29 is all-inclusive: everyone everywhere will grant the Lord the honor and glory due his name.

The imagery for the Lord is majestic and emphasizes his overall awesomeness. The phrase "splendor of his holiness" (v. 2) emphasizes distinctiveness of the Lord as ethically perfect, the one who stands above and beyond creation, and who acts rightly in all circumstances.

Verses 3–9 give the basis for this call to praise. In these verses, the coming of the Lord is portrayed through the imagery of a powerful thunderstorm that is roaring and coming off the sea toward the temple. The thunder is likened to the voice of the Lord. It shatters the silence and echoes out across the waters. In the ancient world, the waters of the sea represented a chaotic and destructive force. Here the Lord's voice in the thunder demonstrates God's superiority over all other forces (vv. 3–4).

In verses 6–9a, the voice of the Lord subdues and strikes mighty trees, nations, and deserts. All of the place names in these verses stand outside of Israel proper. The implication is that the Lord is not merely the true King of Israel, but is indeed the King of all creation. The storm imagery is vivid. Imagine the most severe thunderstorm you've experienced and feel the power of the language here as the psalm helps us to *feel* the coming of the Lord.

Verse 9b gives the only fitting response to the awe-inspiring arrival of the Lord in the storm. All who have gathered cry out, "Glory!" Glory is the perceived awesomeness and weightiness of God's presence. It is an acknowledgment of God's greatness and our smallness in his presence. It is the feeling that we get when we stand before a majestic mountain or a huge waterfall or some other wonder of the world.

Verses 10–11 make explicit the message of the storm imagery. The Lord is King of creation and rules forever. The earth is secure for God's people. The Lord strengthens them and extends his blessings to them.

This psalm invites us to ground our security in the knowledge and assurance that the God of creation is alive and well. He sustains our world, but more important for us as we seek to live faithfully, he promises to sustain us as we journey through this world on mission.

1. What is the meaning of the storm imagery in Psalm 29?

2. According to Psalm 29, why should we be confident about our ultimate security in this world?

3. What does Psalm 29 teach you about the worship and praise of the Lord?

WEEK NINE

GATHERING DISCUSSION OUTLINE

A. Open session in prayer.

B. View video for this week's reading.

C. What general impressions and thoughts do you have after considering the video and reading the daily writings on these Scriptures? What specifically did this week's psalms teach you about faith, life, and prayer?

D. Discuss selected questions from the daily readings.

    1. **KEY OBSERVATION (PSALM 26):** When trouble comes, God's people respond with faithful living and put their hope in God.

    DISCUSSION QUESTION: What role does our faithfulness play in prayer?

    2. **KEY OBSERVATION (PSALM 27):** During times of crisis, God's people turn away from fear and wait expectantly for God to act.

    DISCUSSION QUESTION: Describe the tension between the psalmist's faith and his need to ask the Lord for help. What does this tension teach us about the role of prayer?

    3. **KEY OBSERVATION (PSALM 28):** God provides security for *all* God's people.

    DISCUSSION QUESTION: What images or metaphors for God do you find most meaningful in this psalm? How do these communicate the security that we find in the Lord?

4. **KEY OBSERVATION (PSALM 29):** Praise orients us to the power, greatness, and prestige of the Lord.

   DISCUSSION QUESTION: What language does Psalm 29 use to praise the Lord?

5. **KEY OBSERVATION (PSALM 29):** Everyone everywhere will grant the Lord the honor and glory due his name.

   DISCUSSION QUESTION: What does Psalm 29 teach you about the worship and praise of the Lord?

E. Close session with prayer.

WEEK TEN

Psalms 30–31 and Psalms 33–35

Lament and Gratitude

INTRODUCTION

This week we will study Psalms 30–31 and 33–35. We are skipping Psalm 32 so that we can study it in depth along with Psalm 36 next week.

This block of psalms is important as we begin to reach the end of Book 1 of the Psalter (Psalms 1–41). After the introduction (Psalms 1–2), we encountered mainly a series of laments. These function to teach us how to pray in difficult times by anchoring ourselves to the Lord. The last laments that we read were Psalms 25–28.

Beginning in Psalm 29 there is a shift from lament to praise and thanksgiving. Psalm 29 is a praise hymn to the Lord for his reign as King. Psalms 30–31 are thanksgiving psalms. They testify to the power, ability, and willingness of the Lord to act to save God's people. They serve to remind God's people that the response to salvation is *gratitude*. Life is not the same after experiencing anguish and suffering. When God works to bring hope and healing, God's people continue to pray. But now the prayers focus on giving thanks to the Lord as an act of worship to the Lord but also as a witness and testimony to other believers. The testimony of a grateful heart is a powerful teaching device. It gives hope to others who may be in the midst of lament. It also teaches the community about faithfulness and God's love in the midst of suffering.

As we will see next week, Psalm 32 teaches God's people to pray for forgiveness of sin. This is a lament for times when the problem is internal to the pray-er rather than an external enemy or affliction.

Psalm 33 is a hymn of praise that models the worship of the Lord for who God is and what God has done. It is praise apart from lament or thanksgiving.

It reminds God's people that prayer does not always have to originate with cries for help or with expressions of gratitude for past deliverance. It is also vital to take time to praise the Lord and adore God for his goodness, power, and love.

Psalm 34 takes us back to thanksgiving and continues this week's lesson on praise and gratitude. Psalms 29–34 reorient the lives of God's people around the worship of God as a community of faith. The laments have taught us the importance of finding security in the midst of suffering in a trusting relationship with God. These psalms of praise and thanksgiving remind us of *why* we can trust and rest in the secure arms of the Lord.

The last psalm this week is Psalm 35, which returns us to now-familiar prayer lament. As we move toward the conclusion of our study of Book 1, lament will again dominate the landscape of the Psalter.

ONE
Cultivating Gratitude

Psalm 30 ESV *I will extol you, O Lord, for you have drawn me up and have not let my foes rejoice over me. [2]O Lord my God, I cried to you for help, and you have healed me. [3]O Lord, you have brought up my soul from Sheol; you restored me to life from among those who go down to the pit.*

[4]Sing praises to the Lord, O you his saints, and give thanks to his holy name. [5]For his anger is but for a moment, and his favor is for a lifetime. Weeping may tarry for the night, but joy comes with the morning.

[6]As for me, I said in my prosperity, "I shall never be moved." [7]By your favor, O Lord, you made my mountain stand strong; you hid your face; I was dismayed.

[8]To you, O Lord, I cry, and to the Lord I plead for mercy: [9]"What profit is there in my death, if I go down to the pit? Will the dust praise you? Will it tell of your faithfulness? [10]Hear, O Lord, and be merciful to me! O Lord, be my helper!"

[11]You have turned for me my mourning into dancing; you have loosed my sackcloth and clothed me with gladness, [12]that my glory may sing your praise and not be silent. O Lord my God, I will give thanks to you forever!

Key Observation. Cultivating the attitude and habits of gratitude is critical for the life of faith.

Understanding the Word. Psalm 30 is a thanksgiving psalm. Cultivating the attitude and habits of gratitude is critical for the life of faith. Thanksgiving flows from lament. Thanksgiving is the testimony of a person who has experienced anguish, cried out to the Lord, and witnessed the work of God *personally*. We need to listen to such people. Thanksgiving models the proper response to God's grace. We give thanks and praise to the God who has done for us what no man could have accomplished. The thanksgiving psalm is a witness to the community. To hear another's thanksgiving is to be filled with hope and confidence that God will likewise hear our prayers. Thanksgiving also serves to remind God's people during times of plenty to remain grounded in God as the reason for our abundance.

Psalm 30 contains four movements. Verses 1–3 offer opening praise and thanks to God. Verses 4–5 invite the community to join in the worship. Verses 6–10 narrate the original crisis. Finally, verses 11–12 conclude the psalm with additional praise and thanksgiving.

In verses 1–3, the psalmist rejoiced in his delivered state. God had raised him up. He had faced enemies and was at the brink of death. Yet God thwarted the designs of his opponents and restored him to the fullness of life. Therefore, the psalmist desired to *exalt* God. This is what praise does. It lifts God up over any other being or thing. God is the one who saved the psalmist. He wanted the world to know.

Verses 4–5 remind us that worship is not a solitary act. The psalmist could praise the Lord in a solo performance, but the life of faith involves *community*. The psalmist immediately invited God's people to join in his praise. Verse 5 was the essence of the psalmist's testimony. His time of trouble was over. Night had passed. Morning had come. God had triumphed.

What was the psalmist's story? We don't hear the specifics. This is one of the reasons that the Psalms remain vital and relevant for us. They are specific enough to guide us in our prayers, but remain ambiguous enough that we can find our experiences within them. The psalmist affirmed his deep roots in the faith in verses 6–7a. He recognized that security is found in God alone. His crisis arrived in verse 7b. His life reversed from security to desperation when he experienced a sense of the loss of God's presence. Verse 1 hints that enemies were involved in this crisis.

Verses 8–10 testify to the prayer that the psalmist offered to the Lord. The psalmist turned to God for mercy. Verses 9–10 contain the precise words that the psalmist prayed as he cried out for mercy and help.

God answered his prayer (vv. 11–12). The language of verse 11 reflects the reversal of fortune and the relief experienced by the psalmist. He felt alive and full of joy. The psalmist's experience of divine grace and mercy transformed him from lament to worship and witness. This is important. When God acts on our behalf, we become living testimonies to the world of God's goodness through our praise and thanksgiving.

1. How does Psalm 30 teach us to praise and give thanks for God's mercy and grace?

2. For what are you grateful?

3. What role does our community play in our thanksgiving?

TWO

The Highs and Lows of Faith

Psalm 31 *In you, Lord, I have taken refuge; let me never be put to shame; deliver me in your righteousness. ²Turn your ear to me, come quickly to my rescue; be my rock of refuge, a strong fortress to save me. ³Since you are my rock and my fortress, for the sake of your name lead and guide me. ⁴Keep me free from the trap that is set for me, for you are my refuge. ⁵Into your hands I commit my spirit; deliver me, Lord, my faithful God.*

⁶I hate those who cling to worthless idols; as for me, I trust in the Lord. ⁷I will be glad and rejoice in your love, for you saw my affliction and knew the anguish of my soul. ⁸You have not given me into the hands of the enemy but have set my feet in a spacious place.

⁹Be merciful to me, Lord, for I am in distress; my eyes grow weak with sorrow, my soul and body with grief. ¹⁰My life is consumed by anguish and my years by groaning; my strength fails because of my affliction, and my bones grow weak. ¹¹Because of all my enemies, I am the utter contempt of my neighbors and an object of dread to my closest friends—those who see me on the street flee from

me. ¹²*I am forgotten as though I were dead; I have become like broken pottery.*
¹³*For I hear many whispering, "Terror on every side!" They conspire against me
and plot to take my life.*

¹⁴*But I trust in you, LORD; I say, "You are my God." *¹⁵*My times are in your
hands; deliver me from the hands of my enemies, from those who pursue me.
*¹⁶*Let your face shine on your servant; save me in your unfailing love. *¹⁷*Let me not
be put to shame, LORD, for I have cried out to you; but let the wicked be put to
shame and be silent in the realm of the dead. *¹⁸*Let their lying lips be silenced, for
with pride and contempt they speak arrogantly against the righteous.*

¹⁹*How abundant are the good things that you have stored up for those who
fear you, that you bestow in the sight of all, on those who take refuge in you. *²⁰*In
the shelter of your presence you hide them from all human intrigues; you keep
them safe in your dwelling from accusing tongues.*

²¹*Praise be to the LORD, for he showed me the wonders of his love when I was
in a city under siege. *²²*In my alarm I said, "I am cut off from your sight!" Yet you
heard my cry for mercy when I called to you for help.*

²³*Love the LORD, all his faithful people! The LORD preserves those who are
true to him, but the proud he pays back in full. *²⁴*Be strong and take heart, all you
who hope in the LORD.*

Key Observation. As we follow Jesus into the world and seek to live faithfully
as his witnesses, we will experience both highs and lows.

Understanding the Word. Psalm 31 is difficult to categorize. It is part lament,
part song of trust, and part thanksgiving. Psalm 31 tells a story. It reminds us
that the life of faith is complicated. As we follow Jesus into the world and seek
to live faithfully as his hands, feet, and mouthpieces, we will experience both
highs and lows. This psalm witnesses to these realities.

Psalm 31 opens with a declaration and prayer (vv. 1–5). The psalmist
trusted the Lord. He recognized that the Lord was his refuge. The psalmist was
entirely devoted in terms of commitment. He asked for the Lord's guidance
(v. 3) and entrusted his spirit to the Lord (v. 5). Jesus himself quoted verse 5
on the cross as his final words before dying (Luke 23:46). This is deep trust
indeed. The psalmist asked for deliverance and rescue from an unnamed situation (vv. 1–2, 4).

In verses 6–8, the psalmist witnessed to his faith. He was adamant about his trust and convictions about the way of the Lord. He had refused to seek comfort or help from idols. He confessed that the Lord hears prayers, delivers from difficulties, protects from enemies, and provides a secure and abundant foundation for living well. The psalmist was well acquainted with God. It was clear that he sought to enjoy a moment-by-moment walk with the Lord.

Yet this relationship does not mean that the psalmist would live worry free. Verses 9–18 narrate a challenging time and model a desperate but trusting prayer for help. In verses 9–10, it was clear that the psalmist's plight affected his entire being (inside and out). His vision, body, and soul felt anguish. Relationally, he was lost and experienced the shame and rejection of seemingly everyone: friends, neighbors, and foes (vv. 11–13). He was truly in the depths of despair. If the anguish of feeling abandoned by God was not enough, he experienced the scorn of his fellow men and women.

But his faith remained steadfast. Imagine your own response to this situation. What would you do or say? For the psalmist, there was only one way—the way of the Lord. He continued to proclaim trust and allegiance. "You are my God" he confessed (v. 14). He recognized that only God could save him from the wicked who sought his harm and humiliation.

The Lord does indeed save. This was the psalmist's testimony (vv. 19–24). His time of trouble had passed. His cries for help had turned to impassioned praise and thanksgiving. In the Lord is abundance and goodness (v. 19). The Lord provides refuge and security for his people. This does not inoculate them against times of insecurity, but rather provides an enduring security for the journey of life (vv. 20–22).

Verses 23–24 serve as an exhortation for God's people who have heard the testimony of the psalmist. He called his hearers to love the Lord (cf. Deuteronomy 6:4–5). He reminded them that *faithfulness* pays dividends in the long run. Therefore, God's people should live courageously and act boldly in the present to advance God's mission (v. 24).

1. How does this psalm teach us to pray?

2. How does the psalmist's testimony encourage you in your own faith?

3. What do you hope to model for others in your own journey of faith?

THREE
Worship in All Seasons

Psalm 33 ESV *Shout for joy in the* LORD, *O you righteous! Praise befits the upright.* [2]*Give thanks to the* LORD *with the lyre; make melody to him with the harp of ten strings!* [3]*Sing to him a new song; play skillfully on the strings, with loud shouts.*

[4]*For the word of the* LORD *is upright, and all his work is done in faithfulness.* [5]*He loves righteousness and justice; the earth is full of the steadfast love of the* LORD. [6]*By the word of the* LORD *the heavens were made, and by the breath of his mouth all their host.* [7]*He gathers the waters of the sea as a heap; he puts the deeps in storehouses.*

[8]*Let all the earth fear the* LORD; *let all the inhabitants of the world stand in awe of him!* [9]*For he spoke, and it came to be; he commanded, and it stood firm.*

[10]*The* LORD *brings the counsel of the nations to nothing; he frustrates the plans of the peoples.* [11]*The counsel of the* LORD *stands forever, the plans of his heart to all generations.* [12]*Blessed is the nation whose God is the* LORD, *the people whom he has chosen as his heritage!*

[13]*The* LORD *looks down from heaven; he sees all the children of man;* [14]*from where he sits enthroned he looks out on all the inhabitants of the earth,* [15]*he who fashions the hearts of them all and observes all their deeds.* [16]*The king is not saved by his great army; a warrior is not delivered by his great strength.* [17]*The war horse is a false hope for salvation, and by its great might it cannot rescue.*

[18]*Behold, the eye of the* LORD *is on those who fear him, on those who hope in his steadfast love,* [19]*that he may deliver their soul from death and keep them alive in famine.*

[20]*Our soul waits for the* LORD; *he is our help and our shield.* [21]*For our heart is glad in him, because we trust in his holy name.* [22]*Let your steadfast love, O* LORD, *be upon us, even as we hope in you.*

Key Observation. *Praise* and *worship* are core practices for God's people during all seasons of life.

Understanding the Word. Psalm 33 is a bold hymn of praise to the Lord for who God is and what God has done. It anchors the closing psalms of Book 1

(Psalms 1–41) and orients the lives of God's people around praise. We've seen the language of praise and worship throughout the psalms so far, but the praise has been mixed into prayers focusing mainly on crying out for help or giving thanks for rescue from tumultuous times. Psalm 33 reminds God's people that *praise* and *worship* are core practices during all times. The worship of the Lord is foundational for the life of faith. One of the key issues that we've stressed in our reading of the Psalms thus far is the human need for *security*. Hymns of praise root our security in the Lord and stress our standing with God *before* trouble strikes. Praise and worship provide a framework and structure for our faith that readies us during both good times and bad.

The structure of Psalm 33 supports its emphasis on praise. Its twenty-two verses each begin with a different letter of the Hebrew alphabet. This is the same structure deployed by Psalm 25. It serves to suggest completeness and totality for the message of Psalm 33. It offers a comprehensive look at what it means to praise the Lord. Psalm 33 also divides neatly into two halves: verses 1–11 and 12–22.

The first half of the psalm praises the Lord for his power as Creator. It opens with an invitation to praise (vv. 1–3). These verses echo the language that will conclude the Psalter in Psalms 146–150. It imagines the community of God's people to be a worshiping community.

God's people worship the Lord because of who God is: *faithful* and *loyally loving* (vv. 4–5). These characteristics manifest themselves in his awesome displays of power in creation (vv. 6–11). The Lord stands above the heavens and the earth. The final verdict on creation is that the Lord's good intentions will prevail and stand forever (v. 11). There is no power in all creation that can stand against the Lord. This is good news indeed for the faithful who seek to witness to his love, mercy, and kindness.

How do the people of God live out this good news? It is not with acts of human *power*. Verses 12–22 serve as a clear reminder that our hope is in God alone. It is a blessing to be the Lord's. The Creator God looks down and knows what is happening all over the earth (vv. 13–15). This is the true security that we enjoy as people of faith. But having God with us is not a justification for militarism or trusting in our own strength (vv. 16–17). There is always a temptation to hedge our bets by trusting in *something* or *someone else*: our gifts, talents, military, wealth, etc. This, however, is always the wrong move.

Psalm 33 calls out to us to anchor our hopes and dreams in the ways of the Lord (vv. 18–19). Our Creator is our Savior. His ways lead to life. Our hope is in the audacious biblical promise that love will prevail (v. 18). Jesus' life, death, and resurrection anticipate this and announce God's ultimate victory. Our lives are secure in the Lord's love and serve as testifiers and witnesses to his greatness through our praise and worship.

1. What is the basis for the praise of the Lord in Psalm 33?

2. What role does praise and worship play in the life of followers of Jesus?

3. What are specific features of Psalm 33 that you can adopt in your own praise of the Lord?

FOUR

Remembering to Give Thanks

Psalm 34 *I will extol the Lord at all times; his praise will always be on my lips.* *²I will glory in the Lord; let the afflicted hear and rejoice. ³Glorify the Lord with me; let us exalt his name together.*

⁴I sought the Lord, and he answered me; he delivered me from all my fears. ⁵Those who look to him are radiant; their faces are never covered with shame. ⁶This poor man called, and the Lord heard him; he saved him out of all his troubles. ⁷The angel of the Lord encamps around those who fear him, and he delivers them.

⁸Taste and see that the Lord is good; blessed is the one who takes refuge in him. ⁹Fear the Lord, you his holy people, for those who fear him lack nothing. ¹⁰The lions may grow weak and hungry, but those who seek the Lord lack no good thing. ¹¹Come, my children, listen to me; I will teach you the fear of the Lord. ¹²Whoever of you loves life and desires to see many good days, ¹³keep your tongue from evil and your lips from telling lies. ¹⁴Turn from evil and do good; seek peace and pursue it.

¹⁵The eyes of the Lord are on the righteous, and his ears are attentive to their cry; ¹⁶but the face of the Lord is against those who do evil, to blot out their name from the earth.

[17]The righteous cry out, and the LORD hears them; he delivers them from all their troubles. [18]The LORD is close to the brokenhearted and saves those who are crushed in spirit.

[19]The righteous person may have many troubles, but the LORD delivers him from them all; [20]he protects all his bones, not one of them will be broken.

[21]Evil will slay the wicked; the foes of the righteous will be condemned. [22]The LORD will rescue his servants; no one who takes refuge in him will be condemned.

Key Observation. The Lord will be present with us in both suffering and triumph.

Understanding the Word. Psalm 34 is a thanksgiving prayer with a twist. As we saw with Psalm 30, a thanksgiving psalm serves to cultivate an attitude of gratitude in the hearts and minds of God's people. God's people remember the times when God acted to save them and respond to these memories with thanksgiving and praise. Giving thanks shapes us into *grateful* people. In our day, we often suffer from crises of entitlement—we assume that life is supposed to work out, and when it doesn't we complain or resort to cynicism and bitterness. The book of Psalms testifies to power and love of the Lord to guide God's people through the world as his missional people. Gratitude grounds us in God's love by reminding us of his grace and of our dependence upon it. The twist that Psalm 34 adds is that the psalmist turned from giving thanks to sharing his wisdom with all God's people.

Psalm 34 opens with the psalmist's personal vow to praise the Lord as well as a communal invitation to join in the celebration (vv. 1–3). In particular, the psalmist called on those who were presently afflicted to listen and offer praise (v. 2). The psalmist was about to share his story of deliverance (vv. 4–10) and his mature reflections on life drawn from God's actions (vv. 11–22).

The reason for the opening call to praise was the psalmist's personal testimony of God's grace in action in his life (v. 4). He prayed to the Lord in a time of deep need and God saved him. The psalmist did not share specifics but he was adamant that God is a God who delivers. The psalmist exuded confidence in the security that comes with fearing and knowing the Lord (vv. 5–9). Fear of the Lord is not dread and terror. It is an attitude of wise dependence on God. "The fear of the LORD is the beginning of knowledge" (Prov. 1:7). All of us are afraid of something. The Bible desires to free us from all fear except for fear of the Lord. The good news is this: the only thing that we are to fear is God and God *loves us*. The psalmist thus confidently called his audience to experience God's goodness for themselves (vv. 8–10).

In the second half of the prayer (vv. 11–22), the psalmist shifted to serving as a teacher of wisdom. The Lord is trustworthy and mighty to save. The Lord answers prayer. How then shall we live? The psalmist invited us to ponder his words (v. 11).

The psalmist focused on two realities: (1) the faithful fruit of a life centered on the Lord (vv. 12–14) and (2) the Lord's faithfulness to his people (vv. 15–22). First, our mode of living matters. The Scriptures call us to love God and love others. The psalmist reminded God's people to be forces for good by pursuing peace and harmony. At the most basic level, this involves us avoiding using our speech for ill purposes. We may summarize John Wesley's instructions for the early Methodists in this manner: Do no harm and do go.

Second, the Lord is trustworthy and faithful to protect God's people. We can live lives of holiness because the Lord embodies faithfulness. The psalmist reminded us that God will guide and care for those who seek him (vv. 15, 17). The faithful will experience hardship, but the Lord will be present with them in both suffering and triumph (vv. 18–20, 22). The wicked will experience loss because the way of evil has no future (vv. 16, 21).

1. What role does thanksgiving serve in the life of faith?

2. How does memory help us to express gratitude in our prayers?

3. What kind of person does Psalm 34 call us to become?

FIVE

Praying against Our Enemies

Psalm 35 ESV *Contend, O Lord, with those who contend with me; fight against those who fight against me! [2] Take hold of shield and buckler and rise for my help! [3] Draw the spear and javelin against my pursuers! Say to my soul, "I am your salvation!"*

⁴Let them be put to shame and dishonor who seek after my life! Let them be turned back and disappointed who devise evil against me! ⁵Let them be like chaff before the wind, with the angel of the Lord *driving them away! ⁶Let their way be dark and slippery, with the angel of the* Lord *pursuing them!*

⁷For without cause they hid their net for me; without cause they dug a pit for my life. ⁸Let destruction come upon him when he does not know it! And let the net that he hid ensnare him; let him fall into it—to his destruction!

⁹Then my soul will rejoice in the Lord, exulting in his salvation. ¹⁰All my bones shall say, "O Lord*, who is like you, delivering the poor from him who is too strong for him, the poor and needy from him who robs him?"*

¹¹Malicious witnesses rise up; they ask me of things that I do not know. ¹²They repay me evil for good; my soul is bereft. ¹³But I, when they were sick— I wore sackcloth; I afflicted myself with fasting; I prayed with head bowed on my chest. ¹⁴I went about as though I grieved for my friend or my brother; as one who laments his mother, I bowed down in mourning.

¹⁵But at my stumbling they rejoiced and gathered; they gathered together against me; wretches whom I did not know tore at me without ceasing; ¹⁶like profane mockers at a feast, they gnash at me with their teeth.

¹⁷How long, O Lord*, will you look on? Rescue me from their destruction, my precious life from the lions! ¹⁸I will thank you in the great congregation; in the mighty throng I will praise you.*

¹⁹Let not those rejoice over me who are wrongfully my foes, and let not those wink the eye who hate me without cause. ²⁰For they do not speak peace, but against those who are quiet in the land they devise words of deceit. ²¹They open wide their mouths against me; they say, "Aha, Aha! Our eyes have seen it!"

²²You have seen, O Lord*; be not silent! O* Lord*, be not far from me! ²³Awake and rouse yourself for my vindication, for my cause, my God and my Lord! ²⁴Vindicate me, O* Lord*, my God, according to your righteousness, and let them not rejoice over me! ²⁵Let them not say in their hearts, "Aha, our heart's desire!" Let them not say, "We have swallowed him up."*

²⁶Let them be put to shame and disappointed altogether who rejoice at my calamity! Let them be clothed with shame and dishonor who magnify themselves against me!

²⁷Let those who delight in my righteousness shout for joy and be glad and say evermore, "Great is the Lord*, who delights in the welfare of his servant!" ²⁸Then my tongue shall tell of your righteousness and of your praise all the day long.*

Key Observation. We can relinquish our rage and hurt to the Lord, who is faithful and just to bring about his good future for his people.

Understanding the Word. Psalm 35 is intense. The psalmist was under relentless and ruthless attack from enemies. Psalm 35 is a cry to the Lord for help, but it also takes a path that we have not yet explored in our study. The psalmist asked for help and then prayed vigorously for the undoing of his opponents. As followers of Jesus, we may remember his instructions, "Love your enemies and pray for those who persecute you" (Matt. 5:44). Let's explore the psalmist's lament and reflect on how his words teach us to pray.

Psalm 35 divides into three parts: verses 1–10, 11–18, and 19–28. In the first section, the psalmist opened the prayer with a cry to God requesting that the Lord take up his cause and fight against his enemies (vv. 1–3). Note the military language and imagery as God is depicted as a warrior.

The psalmist then immediately described the ruin that he desired for his enemies (vv. 4–8). How do we, as Christ followers, pray these words without blushing a bit? Is it really okay to desire the harm of another? As you read this psalm, recognize a couple of key insights: (1) the psalmist was powerless and at the mercy of his enemies who sought to harm him, (2) the psalmist knew that God could save him, and (3) the psalmist relinquished the desire for the ruin of his enemies to the Lord. This third point is critical. The psalmist did not take matters into his *own* hands but trusted the Lord. In other words, the psalmist released his feelings to the Lord rather than taking action or bottling his extreme emotions, causing his own body to decay from a burning rage.

Verses 9–10 recognize that it is the Lord alone who saves and praises God for caring for those who are powerless and at the mercy of others.

In verses 11–18, the psalmist returned to his lament. He longed for God to act against his enemies. The psalmist had been faithful, including praying and fasting for his enemies when they were ill (vv. 13–14), but at the first opportunity, his enemies relentlessly oppressed him (vv. 15–16). The psalmist pled for help (v. 17) and vowed to witness to the deliverance of the Lord to the community (v. 18).

In the closing section (vv. 19–28), the psalmist continued to move between prayers for deliverance and requests for the demise of his enemies. Yet he remained steadfast in his hope of salvation. He knew that the Lord is just and would do what was right to vindicate him. The psalm closes (vv. 27–28) with the psalmist anticipating communal praise and rejoicing for deliverance. The psalmist envisioned a dramatic shift from being a desperate lamenter in need of salvation to one whose mouth announced to the world the goodness, justice, and righteousness of the Lord who did not leave his faithful servant in distress.

As you ponder the words of Psalm 35, observe its rawness. The psalmist was able to share out of the depths of his being. This is a model prayer. As Christ followers, we do not desire to gloat over the demise of our enemies, but this psalm teaches us how to pray when we find ourselves alone and at the mercy of enemies. We can relinquish our rage and hurt to the only being who is capable of sorting through the messes of life and acting righteously to bring about his good future for his people.

1. How does the intensity of Psalm 35 teach us to pray when we are under assault?

2. What is the significance of the psalmist's prayers *against* his enemies?

3. How can we understand the violence in Psalm 35 as followers of Jesus?

WEEK TEN

GATHERING DISCUSSION OUTLINE

A. Open session in prayer.

B. View video for this week's reading.

C. What general impressions and thoughts do you have after considering the video and reading the daily writings on these Scriptures? What specifically did this week's psalms teach you about faith, life, and prayer?

D. Discuss selected questions from the daily readings.

1. **KEY OBSERVATION (PSALM 30):** Cultivating the attitude and habits of gratitude is critical for the life of faith.

   DISCUSSION QUESTION: How does Psalm 30 teach us to praise and give thanks for God's mercy and grace? For what are you grateful?

2. **KEY OBSERVATION (PSALM 31):** As we follow Jesus into the world and seek to live faithfully as his witnesses, we will experience both highs and lows.

   DISCUSSION QUESTION: How does the psalmist's testimony encourage you in your own faith?

3. **KEY OBSERVATION (PSALM 33):** *Praise* and *worship* are core practices for God's people during all seasons of life.

   DISCUSSION QUESTION: What roles do praise and worship play in the life of followers of Jesus?

4. **KEY OBSERVATION (PSALM 34):** The Lord will be present with us in both suffering and triumph.

   DISCUSSION QUESTION: What advice did the psalmist have for his hearers in Psalm 34?

5. **KEY OBSERVATION (PSALM 35):** We can relinquish our rage and hurt to the Lord, who is faithful and just to bring about his good future for his people.

   DISCUSSION QUESTION: What is the significance of the psalmist's prayers *against* his enemies? How can we understand the violence in Psalm 35 as followers of Jesus?

E. Close session with prayer.

WEEK ELEVEN

Psalms 32 and 36

Sin, Forgiveness, and the Beauty of God

INTRODUCTION

One of the presuppositions of Scripture is that humanity is lost apart from the grace, love, and kindness of God. God's grace and love manifest most fully in the life, death, and resurrection of Jesus our Messiah. Due to human sin, we all find ourselves living with the fruit of our own actions as well as the actions of others (past and present). Sin manifests itself in guilt, shame, alienation, brokenness, and injustice. God's mission is to reverse the results of sin by creating a missional people through whom God will bless the nations (see Genesis 12:3; Exodus 19:5–6; and 1 Peter 2:9). The risen Jesus sends us into this world. Paul summarized the plight and possibility of our world this way: "For all have sinned and fall short of the glory of God, and all are justified freely by his grace through the redemption that came by Christ Jesus" (Rom. 3:23–24).

How do we pray as we seek to live faithfully in our lost and fallen world? Psalms 32 and 36 focus on human sin and wickedness. They address this issue from two different perspectives. Both are psalms of lament, but they have different intentions.

Psalm 32 is a lament for the forgiveness of sin. It serves a key role in the Psalter by teaching us how to pray when we act unfaithfully and find ourselves in need of God's forgiving grace. Psalm 32 models a prayer of confession so that we can experience God's cleansing grace anew and refocus our lives on God's mission.

Psalm 36 is a lament about wickedness. It is similar to Psalm 1 in its stark contrast of two diametrically opposed ways of making it through the world.

Psalm 36:1–4 paints a dark and bleak picture of the world and humanity apart from God's grace. It locates the cause of sin in self-centeredness. Self-centered living plagues men and women. No good comes from this way of life.

In contrast, the second half of the psalm focuses on the beauty and love of the Lord. Sin, self-centeredness, and alienation do not have to be the final verdict on life. In fact, it is pointless and illogical in contrast to the lavishness of God's grace, love, and faithfulness that is freely available to all who seek the Lord.

As we reflect carefully on these two psalms this week, we have an opportunity to ponder sin on one hand and God's love and grace on the other. Both are present in the world, but only God's love will be for all eternity. What would it look like for you to settle the issue of sin and begin to align yourself fully with the love and grace of the Lord?

ONE

Open to Forgiveness

Psalm 32:1–5 *Blessed is the one whose transgressions are forgiven, whose sins are covered. ²Blessed is the one whose sin the* LORD *does not count against them and in whose spirit is no deceit.*

³When I kept silent, my bones wasted away through my groaning all day long. ⁴For day and night your hand was heavy on me; my strength was sapped as in the heat of summer.

⁵Then I acknowledged my sin to you and did not cover up my iniquity. I said, "I will confess my transgressions to the LORD.*" And you forgave the guilt of my sin.*

Key Observation. When we recognize our faults and flaws, we open ourselves up to the forgiveness of God.

Understanding the Word. Psalm 32 is a lament psalm that serves to teach us how to pray for forgiveness. It is the second of the traditional penitential psalms that we introduced with Psalm 6. (The others are Psalms 38, 51, 102, 130, and 143.) Psalm 32 offers profound reflection on sin and forgiveness in its two parts: verses 1–5 and 6–11. It also includes the role of the community of faith in the process of sin, confession, and forgiveness.

Verses 1–2 open Psalm 32 with two related beatitudes. This is a psalm about being happy. This is a theme of the Psalter. We've seen the word *happy* (translated as "blessed") in our readings of Psalms 1:1, 2:12, and 146:5. *Happy* means living in a state of God's blessing.

What is indicative of being in a state of God-given blessing according to Psalm 32? It is the experience of *forgiveness* of sin. Verses 1–2 reflect on a life of grace: the blessing of forgiveness and a life marked by faithfulness in response to God's grace. This psalm invites its pray-ers to reflect on their lives before God and their community to be sensitive to their brokenness and bring their sins and failures to the only source of cleansing: the Lord.

Verses 1–2 make three statements about sin and forgiveness. The psalmist used three different words for sin: *transgression, sin,* and *iniquity.* The psalmist also deployed three different verbs for God's response to sin: *forgiven, covered,* and *does not impute.* The richness of the vocabulary reminds us of the seriousness of the problem. Psalm 36:1–4, which we will look at this week, likewise offers a broad description of sin. Sin is serious business. God calls us to love him and love others (including ourselves). Sin is the totality of acts and motivations that move us away from living fully as the people whom God created us to be. Sin finds its root in self-will apart from living moment by moment in relationship with God. It involves outright acts of rebellion and times when we miss the mark (intentional or unintentional). It also includes an attitude or will that continually intends or desires a path contrary to God's loving ways.

Brokenness is part of all of our stories. Sin drags on us. It hurts us. It weighs on us in the depths of our beings. Verses 3–4 describe the psalmist's own testimony of sin's effects. Yet this psalm contains good news. God does not leave us in our struggles, alienations, and despair due to our sin. God acts to *cleanse* us.

What does it take to experience God's cleansing? All it takes is voicing our *need* for God. In verse 5, the psalmist modeled the response of the faithful: *confession* and *acknowledgment* to God. When we recognize our faults and flaws, this opens us up for the work of God in our lives. The psalmist testified that God had indeed forgiven him.

1. What does Psalm 32 teach us about the "happy" life?

2. How does Psalm 32 teach us to confess our sins to God?

3. What role does the confession of sin play in your walk with God today?

TWO

Faithful Love

Psalm 32:6–11 *Therefore let all the faithful pray to you while you may be found; surely the rising of the mighty waters will not reach them. ⁷You are my hiding place; you will protect me from trouble and surround me with songs of deliverance.*

⁸I will instruct you and teach you in the way you should go; I will counsel you with my loving eye on you. ⁹Do not be like the horse or the mule, which have no understanding but must be controlled by bit and bridle or they will not come to you. ¹⁰Many are the woes of the wicked, but the LORD's unfailing love surrounds the one who trusts in him.

¹¹Rejoice in the LORD and be glad, you righteous; sing, all you who are upright in heart!

Key Observation. The Lord's committed and faithful love abides with all who trust and find true security in him.

Understanding the Word. The second half of Psalm 32 serves as a witness to the community about good news of forgiveness. Verse 6 opens with an exhortation to all in faithful relationship with God to continue to pray. The apostle Paul will later advise some of the earliest Christians, "Pray continually" (1 Thess. 5:17). Prayer connects us with God. We abide in God through prayer. The Psalter has explored prayers of praise and prayers for help. Prayers of confession remind us that we must stay in relationship with God *even when we have created the mess that surrounds us.*

The faithful will find security with God. The psalmist moved from exhortation to the faithful to direct address of God. God secured the psalmist's future *despite* the sins that he committed and confessed. This does not mean that the psalmist escaped any consequences. He hinted at them in verses 3–4. But our text does declare the consequences are finite in comparison with God's infinite capacity to forgive and create a new future for the psalmist. This is good news for the psalmist and for us!

Verses 8–9 introduce a new voice to the psalm. In these verses, someone from the community, perhaps a priest, spoke wise counsel and instruction into the psalmist's life. This was a critical component for the psalmist as he lived into the experience of forgiveness and restoration. There were reasons for wrong behavior and actions. If the root causes of sin are not addressed, we can easily turn them into recurring patterns. As part of the experience of forgiveness that Psalm 32 describes, the community came alongside of the forgiven psalmist to provide guidance so that the psalmist did not embody the worst characteristics of a horse or mule—a lack of understanding. The Christian faith is not a solitary adventure. God's people exist to serve as a missional *community* that reflects God's character. Our sins mute our witness to the world. As a community of faith we need each other's support, prayers, and guidance as we seek to follow Jesus into the world on mission. Verses 8–9 invite us to listen to our community at the times of our own deep need for forgiveness.

Verses 10–11 bring Psalm 32 to a conclusion by announcing a sure foundation for living our lives. The psalmist briefly mentioned the challenges and woes of the wicked. If we choose to live in our sins, we will experience hardships. This is true for *all* people. But there is good news: the Lord's committed and faithful love abides with all who trust and find true security in the Lord. When we choose the way of faith and faithfulness, we are able to live in the joy that verse 11 invites us to embody. Our rejoicing serves as a testimony to the watching world.

1. Who in my life supports me in my walk with God?

2. How does Psalm 32 describe the pathway to joy?

3. How does Psalm 32 invite us to witness to the world?

THREE

The Danger of the Self

Psalm 36:1–4 *I have a message from God in my heart concerning the sinfulness of the wicked: There is no fear of God before their eyes.*
²In their own eyes they flatter themselves too much to detect or hate their sin.
³The words of their mouths are wicked and deceitful; they fail to act wisely or do good. ⁴Even on their beds they plot evil; they commit themselves to a sinful course and do not reject what is wrong.

Key Observation. The essence of sin is dependence on our thoughts, plans, will, and talents apart from the will of God.

Understanding the Word. Psalm 32 helps us to pray when we find ourselves in need of God's forgiveness. The Lord is a God who forgives. This is good news.

Psalm 36 offers two ways of life. The way of the wicked (vv. 1–4) and one rooted in the love of God (vv. 5–9). These pathways stand in stark contrast. These contrasting portraits of life exist side-by-side in our prayer without any transition between the two. We've encountered the two paths in a couple of ways already during our study. Psalms 1 and 146 describe the ways of the righteous and the ways of the wicked. We've also seen the voice of the psalmist through the lament psalms claiming personal innocence and connection with God. Psalm 36 enriches and deepens these previous black-and-white modes of thinking. Psalm 36 invites those who will learn to pray it to take a look inside and decide whether to align with a life rooted in self or with the expansive love of the Lord.

Verse 1 announces that the psalmist had received a message from God. The psalmist shared the content of this message in verses 1–4. It is a description of what drives a person to commit sin. The vocabulary of sin and evil is rich in these four verses. English translations struggle to capture the nuances. The psalmist used just about every Hebrew word for sin available to paint a broad and jarring picture of life apart from faithfulness and love.

Verse 1b roots sin in a lack of *fear* or *dread* of God. What is lacking in a person who embraces the way of wickedness and rebellion is a sense of one's place in creation. We might say that the person needs a reality check. God does not desire us to be terrified of him. Instead, we are to show a respect and submission to God as Ruler and Judge of creation. The wicked live without regard for any force, person, or power outside of themselves.

Verse 2 continues the description. We find the second occurrence of "eyes." This points to the cause of sin. The wicked justify their actions apart from any external reference point. We would call this being *self-centered*. The heart of sin is living out of our own thoughts, plans, will, and talents. When we set our own standards and are accountable only to ourselves, we lose the ability and self-awareness to detect our brokenness and sinful desires. When this reality manifests itself in the masses, chaos ensues as every individual acts only out of self-interest rather than in a way of life shaped by a love for God and others.

Verses 3–4 focus on the mess created by unfiltered and unbridled self-will and self-centeredness. There is a loss of wise living and speaking. A sense of the common good is nowhere to be found. Their plans and intentions flow out of their selfishness. This makes it impossible for them to walk down a good pathway. If there is a choice for good or evil, they gravitate toward the way of wickedness.

1. How do verses 1–4 describe sin?

2. What are the results of sin according to Psalm 36:1–4?

3. What warning do these verses offer to those who would follow after Jesus?

FOUR

The Beauty of the Lord

Psalm 36:5–9 *Your love,* Lord, *reaches to the heavens, your faithfulness to the skies.* ⁶*Your righteousness is like the highest mountains, your justice like the great deep. You,* Lord, *preserve both people and animals.* ⁷*How priceless is your unfailing love, O God! People take refuge in the shadow of your wings.* ⁸*They feast on the abundance of your house; you give them drink from your river of delights.* ⁹*For with you is the fountain of life; in your light we see light.*

Key Observation. The Lord possesses an immeasurable and limitless quantity of love, righteousness, faithfulness, and justice.

Understanding the Word. If verses 1–4 paint a picture of self-centered human ugliness, the portrait found in verses 5–9 is stunning in its description of the beauty and majesty of God. There are two ways of living described in Psalm 36, but there is really no choice. Read through verses 5–9 again. The imagery is breathtaking. When we close our eyes and imagine how we would describe a good and kind God, it would be a challenge to exceed the wondrous description in these five verses.

First, the psalmist addressed God *personally* as Lord for the initial time in this psalm. The psalmist did not want us to forget that he is not talking about some generic god. He is talking about the Lord.

Then, the psalmist voiced four core attributes of God (vv. 5–6a): love, faithfulness, righteousness, and justice. The stress is on the breadth and immensity of these. The Lord possesses an immeasurable and limitless quantity of them. The God to whom we pray acts out of a loyal love that is faithful to all of his commitments and relationships. God always does the right thing at the right time every time. These virtues and attributes describe the world that God is bringing about through his mission. Notice the focus on *relational* qualities. Love, faithfulness, righteousness, and justice all manifest themselves in relationship between God and others. This is the exact opposite of the mode of life of the wicked. Their focus is on self; the Lord's focus is for the good of creation.

Verse 6b declares the full implication of the Lord's love, faithfulness, righteousness, and justice. Our translation reads, "You, Lord, preserve both people and animals." The word *preserve* is more often translated *save* or *deliver*. The Lord is a god who preserves and/or saves people and animals. God's commitment to relational wholeness means that God cares about people and animals.

This truth is life-giving. "Unfailing love" is the same word in Hebrew as "love" in verse 5. This is the core dimension of God's personality and character. It is affirmed in both Old and New Testaments that God is love (cf. Exodus 34:6 and 1 John 4:16). Humanity can find true refuge and protection in the "shadow of [his] wings" (Ps. 36:7). This is a reference to the Jerusalem temple. This does not mean that God's protection is confined to one place. The temple is a symbol of God's refuge that is universally available to all who know him.

Verses 8–9 emphasize the extravagant abundance available to those who seek refuge in the Lord. The vocabulary invites us to imagine that we are feasting and drinking at God's table. The portions are endless and the very best that are available. If the portrait of wickedness is dark and pointless, the abundance of God is about *life* and *light*. The Lord is love. Life as God intends is beautiful and rich. In John 10:10, Jesus put it this way, "I have come that they may have life, and have it to the full."

1. How do verses 5–9 describe the Lord?

2. How does this description contrast with that of the wicked in verses 1–4?

3. Which of these contrasting portraits of life do you want to embrace?

FIVE

Experiencing the Lord's Faithful Love

Psalm 36:10–12 *Continue your love to those who know you, your righteousness to the upright in heart.* *[11]May the foot of the proud not come against me, nor the hand of the wicked drive me away.* *[12]See how the evildoers lie fallen—thrown down, not able to rise!*

Key Observation. The goal of our witness is to invite the world to experience the self-giving love and justice of God.

Understanding the Word. The psalmist had reached the point of decision. Up to this point, Psalm 36 has described two distinct and contrasting ways of living.

Verses 1–4 center life on decisions and whims of each individual. In the world of verses 1–4, there is a temptation to believe falsely that each man or woman can cut his or her own path through the world as he or she pleases. This is the root of idolatry and injustice. The biblical vision for authentic living flows out of a love for God, people, and all creation. In other words, life moves away from self to focus on relationship. Sin and wickedness result from attempting to shape the world to serve and please us. This is what self-centeredness means. We attempt to live as God. To work out of this framework is to work against the beautiful and just world that God desires and is working to create.

Verses 5–9 offer a robust and stunning countercultural alternative to the way of the wicked. This way of life centers on the one true God—the Lord. The Lord embodies and models relational wholeness by acting in love, faithfulness, righteousness, and justice. God's mission involves saving and preserving all life. God offers all creation security in the present and for all eternity.

So the readers of Psalm 36 must face key questions: In what mode of living will we find our center? Is life all about us? Or does true life arise out of a dynamic relationship with the Lord of love, faithfulness, righteousness, and justice? At some level this decision is obvious. But will we consciously take this decision and align our lives with the Lord?

In verses 10–12, the psalmist modeled a prayer in favor of the way of the Lord of infinite love. Verse 10 makes the psalmist's choice clear. He recognized the Lord's way and asked the Lord to continue to cause love and righteousness to abound for those in relationship with the Lord. In other words, he prayed, "Lord, continue to be the God of abundance that you revealed to me in verses 5–9."

This is a countercultural choice and remains so today. It is risky to live freely for the sake of others. To privilege a love for God and neighbor over the self-centeredness of the modern (and ancient) world puts us into a position where we can be hurt, used, or manipulated by those who choose the pathway of self-will (vv. 1–4). This is the reason that Psalm 36 shifts to a prayer for protection from the wicked in verses 11–12. This is not a prayer *against* the world as much as it is a prayer *for* those who desire to live a self-giving life of love and justice in alignment with the character of God (vv. 5–9) and modeled by Jesus in the Gospels. The goal of our witness is to invite the world to experience this truest expression of human life.

1. How do you embody God's way of life in your interactions with God and the world?

2. For what, specifically, is the psalmist asking in verses 10–12? How can this inform us in our own prayers?

3. How does the psalmist bring the portrayal of the two ways of life to a climax in his closing petition to God (vv. 10–12)?

WEEK ELEVEN

GATHERING DISCUSSION OUTLINE

A. Open session in prayer.

B. View video for this week's reading.

C. What general impressions and thoughts do you have after considering the video and reading the daily writings on these Scriptures? What specifically did this week's psalms teach you about faith, life, and prayer? What would it look like for you to settle the issue of sin and begin to align yourself fully with the love and grace of the Lord?

D. Discuss selected questions from the daily readings.

1. KEY OBSERVATION (PSALM 32:1–5): When we recognize our faults and flaws, we open ourselves up to the forgiveness of God.

DISCUSSION QUESTION: What role does the confession of sin play in your walk with God?

2. KEY OBSERVATION (PSALM 32:6–11): The Lord's committed and faithful love abides with all who trust and find true security in him.

DISCUSSION QUESTION: How does Psalm 32 describe the pathway to joy?

3. KEY OBSERVATION (PSALM 36:1–4): The essence of sin is dependence on our thoughts, plans, will, and talents apart from the will of God.

DISCUSSION QUESTION: How do verses 1–4 describe sin?

4. **KEY OBSERVATION (PSALM 36:5–9):** The Lord possesses an immeasurable and limitless quantity of love, righteousness, faithfulness, and justice.

   DISCUSSION QUESTION: How do verses 5–9 describe the Lord? How does this description contrast with that of the wicked in verses 1–4?

5. **KEY OBSERVATION (PSALM 36:10–12):** The goal of our witness is to invite the world to experience the self-giving love and justice of God.

   DISCUSSION QUESTION: How do you embody God's way of life in your interactions with God and the world?

E. Close session with prayer.

WEEK TWELVE

Psalms 37–41

Faithfulness, Dependence, and Mission

INTRODUCTION

We have arrived at the final week of our study of Book 1 of the Psalms (Psalms 1–41). Let us review our journey. The book of Psalms is the prayer book for God's missional people. One of our assumptions in reading the Psalms is that each of us is seeking to follow Jesus into our world to serve as his hands, feet, and mouthpieces. Following Jesus involves a deep trust in Jesus' life, death, and resurrection as our foundation. Living as a follower of Jesus manifests itself in a life of love for God and love for others.

Such a lifestyle serves as a witness and testimony to both believers and those who do not yet follow Jesus. But this way of life must be cultivated and fed. The book of Psalms serves as our companion for the journey of faith. It is a rich resource for praying and worshiping the Lord during all seasons of our lives.

As we saw in the initial two weeks, the book of Psalms begins and ends with a grounding vision to orient us (Psalms 1–2) and a concluding climax of praise to encourage us (Psalms 146–150). We can make our way through the world and enjoy the happy life by rooting ourselves in Scripture (Psalm 1) and in the hope of a secure future guaranteed by the Lord's Messiah (Psalm 2). The secure future envisioned by the Psalter involves the full recognition of the Lord as the true King and unending worship of the Lord for who he is and what he has done by all creation (Psalms 146–150).

The book of Psalms proclaims a glorious future hope, but it does not do so at the expense of the challenges of living faithfully *today*. The psalmists who penned the prayers were intimately acquainted with the joys and the sorrows that life brings. They were also personally aware of the opposition and hostility that the faithful will encounter from those who do not share the values of God's kingdom or feel threatened by it.

Beginning with Psalm 3, we encountered the first of many lament psalms or prayers for help and deliverance. The lament is the most common type of prayer in the Psalter. As we've learned, these do not flow from a lack of faith but from a deep trust in the Lord. The implication of so many laments clustering in the initial book of Psalms is this: *although the future of the faithful is secure, life will often seem excruciatingly challenging in the present.* Thus, the laments serve as a gift from God to use as followers of Jesus so that we do not grow weak in our faith and have model prayers to pray when we may lack our own words. Moreover, the laments serve to remind us of our brothers and sisters around the world who may be suffering even when we are not personally in the midst of trials.

If laments dominate Book 1, they are not the only witness to prayer. We've also encountered psalms reminding us of the need to praise the Lord in worship (Psalm 8), of our security in God's Messiah (Psalm 18), of the important role that Scripture plays (Psalm 19), of our deep trust in the Lord (Psalm 23), and of the crucial need to give thanks to God for answered prayer (Psalm 30).

The final five psalms of Book 1 (Psalms 37–41) serve as a fitting conclusion to the first of the Psalter's five books (1–41, 42–72, 73–89, 90–106, and 107–150). Psalm 37 is a psalm that focuses on teaching the ways of the Lord as the only fitting pathway for our journey. Psalms 38–39 offer final laments. Then Psalms 40–41 conclude Book 1 by referencing the happy life (40:4 and 41:1; cf. 1:1 and 2:12) and then modeling thanksgiving to the Lord for his guidance and deliverance through the world.

ONE
Living the Good Life

Psalm 37 *Do not fret because of those who are evil or be envious of those who do wrong; ²for like the grass they will soon wither, like green plants they will soon die away.*

³Trust in the LORD and do good; dwell in the land and enjoy safe pasture. ⁴Take delight in the LORD, and he will give you the desires of your heart.

⁵*Commit your way to the LORD; trust in him and he will do this:* ⁶*He will make your righteous reward shine like the dawn, your vindication like the noonday sun.*

⁷*Be still before the LORD and wait patiently for him; do not fret when people succeed in their ways, when they carry out their wicked schemes.*

⁸*Refrain from anger and turn from wrath; do not fret—it leads only to evil.* ⁹*For those who are evil will be destroyed, but those who hope in the LORD will inherit the land.*

¹⁰*A little while, and the wicked will be no more; though you look for them, they will not be found.* ¹¹*But the meek will inherit the land and enjoy peace and prosperity.*

¹²*The wicked plot against the righteous and gnash their teeth at them;* ¹³*but the Lord laughs at the wicked, for he knows their day is coming.*

¹⁴*The wicked draw the sword and bend the bow to bring down the poor and needy, to slay those whose ways are upright.* ¹⁵*But their swords will pierce their own hearts, and their bows will be broken.*

¹⁶*Better the little that the righteous have than the wealth of many wicked;* ¹⁷*for the power of the wicked will be broken, but the LORD upholds the righteous.*

¹⁸*The blameless spend their days under the LORD's care, and their inheritance will endure forever.* ¹⁹*In times of disaster they will not wither; in days of famine they will enjoy plenty.*

²⁰*But the wicked will perish: Though the LORD's enemies are like the flowers of the field, they will be consumed, they will go up in smoke.*

²¹*The wicked borrow and do not repay, but the righteous give generously;* ²²*those the LORD blesses will inherit the land, but those he curses will be destroyed.*

²³*The LORD makes firm the steps of the one who delights in him;* ²⁴*though he may stumble, he will not fall, for the LORD upholds him with his hand.*

²⁵*I was young and now I am old, yet I have never seen the righteous forsaken or their children begging bread.* ²⁶*They are always generous and lend freely; their children will be a blessing.*

²⁷*Turn from evil and do good; then you will dwell in the land forever.* ²⁸*For the LORD loves the just and will not forsake his faithful ones.*

Wrongdoers will be completely destroyed; the offspring of the wicked will perish. ²⁹*The righteous will inherit the land and dwell in it forever.*

³⁰*The mouths of the righteous utter wisdom, and their tongues speak what is just.* ³¹*The law of their God is in their hearts; their feet do not slip.*

³²The wicked lie in wait for the righteous, intent on putting them to death; ³³but the LORD will not leave them in the power of the wicked or let them be condemned when brought to trial.

³⁴Hope in the LORD and keep his way. He will exalt you to inherit the land; when the wicked are destroyed, you will see it.

³⁵I have seen a wicked and ruthless man flourishing like a luxuriant native tree, ³⁶but he soon passed away and was no more; though I looked for him, he could not be found.

³⁷Consider the blameless, observe the upright; a future awaits those who seek peace. ³⁸But all sinners will be destroyed; there will be no future for the wicked.

³⁹The salvation of the righteous comes from the LORD; he is their stronghold in time of trouble. ⁴⁰The LORD helps them and delivers them; he delivers them from the wicked and saves them, because they take refuge in him.

Key Observation. We live faithfully by practicing goodness to others and placing our hope in God

Understanding the Word. Psalm 37 anchors the final five psalms of Book 1 by offering a prayer of instruction for God's people. It teaches about the problem of suffering and evil in the life of faith. Rather than offering a philosophical reflection on why evil persists, the psalmist wrote about the power of faithfulness and the true security that is found only in the way of the Lord. Much of Psalm 37 reads as a collection of proverbial sayings about God's trustworthiness and human faithfulness. Psalm 37 thus serves to expand on the themes that we've encountered consistently in the lament psalms of Book 1.

The psalmist opened with a reflection on the apparent prosperity of the wicked in the present (vv. 1–11). The opening eleven verses lay out the themes that will recur throughout Psalm 37. Evil and evildoers are real. This cannot be denied and people of faith will come into conflict with both. However, the response of the faithful is to turn to the Lord with *trust* (vv. 3, 5), *delight* (v. 4), and *hope* (v. 9). In the book of Romans, Paul offered these words: "Love must be sincere. Hate what is evil; cling to what is good" (Rom. 12:9) and "Do not repay anyone evil for evil" (Rom. 12:17). The psalmist advocated the same strategy. In the face of wickedness, God's people must live faithfully. The Lord will vindicate God's people, but those who practice evil will have no future.

In verses 12–20 the psalmist described the future of the wicked despite their present prosperity. They appear successful because of their ability to scheme and plot (v. 12), their access to weapons (vv. 14–15), their wealth (v. 16), and power (v. 17). These give them the appearance of *self-reliance*. But the psalmist knew better. His advice was clear. Trust in the Lord. The Lord is more powerful than any human claim, talent, or possession. Moreover the Lord sides with the faithful (vv. 13, 17–20).

In verses 21–26, the psalmist expanded his description of faithfulness by prescribing *generosity* as a core trait for God's people to embody. Living faithfully in a difficult world does not mean living out of scarcity and hoarding possessions. God's people exist as a blessing to the world. This implies that they understand wealth and possessions as the means of blessing others. Therefore, they can share and practice acts of generosity without worrying that they will experience lack or want (cf. Psalm 23:1). As we seek to serve as God's missional people, we witness to God's generosity by sharing wealth and possessions with others, especially those in need.

Psalm 37 concludes with a final series of exhortations to practice faithful living (vv. 27–40). The psalmist gave two core instructions: do good (v. 27) and hope in the Lord (v. 34). By doing good, the psalmist meant embracing a lifestyle rooted in the Torah of God (v. 31; cf. Psalms 1 and 19) and speaking wise and just words to others (v. 30). The hope that the psalmist advocated finds its foundation in the future security of the righteous and the lack of future for those lives standing in opposition to God's kingdom.

Verses 39–40 are the climax of the psalm. The psalmist reiterated that the Lord is the source of salvation for God's people and the only true anchor upon which to find security in the world.

1. How did the psalmist attempt to inspire God's people?

2. Why did the psalmist believe that faithfulness mattered?

3. What faithful practices can you embrace that may serve as a positive witness to the world about God's ways?

TWO

Healing and Forgiveness

Psalm 38 Lord, *do not rebuke me in your anger or discipline me in your wrath.*
²Your arrows have pierced me, and your hand has come down on me. ³Because of your wrath there is no health in my body; there is no soundness in my bones because of my sin. ⁴My guilt has overwhelmed me like a burden too heavy to bear.

⁵My wounds fester and are loathsome because of my sinful folly. ⁶I am bowed down and brought very low; all day long I go about mourning. ⁷My back is filled with searing pain; there is no health in my body. ⁸I am feeble and utterly crushed; I groan in anguish of heart.

⁹All my longings lie open before you, Lord; my sighing is not hidden from you. ¹⁰My heart pounds, my strength fails me; even the light has gone from my eyes. ¹¹My friends and companions avoid me because of my wounds; my neighbors stay far away. ¹²Those who want to kill me set their traps, those who would harm me talk of my ruin; all day long they scheme and lie.

¹³I am like the deaf, who cannot hear, like the mute, who cannot speak; ¹⁴I have become like one who does not hear, whose mouth can offer no reply. ¹⁵Lord, I wait for you; you will answer, Lord my God. ¹⁶For I said, "Do not let them gloat or exalt themselves over me when my feet slip."

¹⁷For I am about to fall, and my pain is ever with me. ¹⁸I confess my iniquity; I am troubled by my sin. ¹⁹Many have become my enemies without cause; those who hate me without reason are numerous. ²⁰Those who repay my good with evil lodge accusations against me, though I seek only to do what is good.

²¹Lord, do not forsake me; do not be far from me, my God. ²²Come quickly to help me, my Lord and my Savior.

Key Observation. God's people are able to bring their brokenness and sin to the Lord so that he can forgive, heal, and empower them to serve as witnesses to the world.

Understanding the Word. Psalm 38 plays a crucial role in the flow of the Psalter as we approach the end of Book 1. Psalm 38 is the third lament in Book 1 that models how God's people may confess their sins and seek forgiveness from the Lord (see Psalms 6 and 32). As such, it is an appropriate prayer to follow the instruction found in Psalm 37. Psalm 37 advocates the ongoing faithfulness of God's people rooted in a trusting hope in God's goodness. God's people find true security in the Lord alone. But what happens when God's people do not live faithfully? Is there a way back? Psalm 38 teaches us to pray in such situations.

Psalm 38 opens with the psalmist in absolute despair (vv. 1–3). He pled for the Lord's mercy due to his sin. The psalmist was suffering mental, spiritual, and physical anguish because of his actions. Sin does this to us. The psalmist felt its heaviness in the form of guilt and despair when he recognized that he had betrayed the Lord as well as the community.

Verses 4–8 describe the serious physical reactions that he experiences in his suffering. He was truly in need of the experience of God's grace. The gravity of the psalmist's plight is both a warning to us as God's people about the consequences of sin, but also an encouragement to turn to the only one who can forgive and cleanse us of our sins.

The psalmist again petitioned God (vv. 9–10) in the midst of his suffering (vv. 11–14). The psalmist was an open book before God. The psalmist's situation worsened because he also experienced the shunning and scorn of his community. They avoided him because of his actions.

In verses 15–20, the psalmist began to move his prayer to a conclusion. Notice his focus. Verse 15 shows his steadfastness. He recognized that his sin is the problem, but his faith empowered him to wait expectantly for God to answer him. There was nowhere else for him to turn. The psalmist openly confessed his *sin* problem. *His* sin and not anyone else's was the cause of his troubles and suffering. Others had harmed the psalmist, but he had to take 100 percent responsibility for his own actions.

Psalm 38 ends with a final prayer to the Lord. The psalmist asked God not to forsake him and to help him. Notice the closing words. The psalmist addressed the Lord as his Lord and Savior. God is the true sovereign guide in his life and the one who brings salvation.

Did the psalmist receive the forgiveness for which he pled? The psalm ends without resolution, but given its place in Israel's book of prayers, the answer is yes. This is the testimony of the Bible. The Creator God is a God who is merciful and forgiving (see Exodus 34:6–7a). When we own up to who we are and what we've done, we put ourselves in a posture of openness to receive all that God has for us. It is not God's will that we sin, but God provides a way back. In the New Testament, this way is a person: Jesus the Messiah, the Son of God. Paul wrote these words: "For all have sinned and fall short of the glory of God, and are all justified freely by his grace through the redemption that came by Christ Jesus" (Rom. 3:23–24). John wrote, "If we confess our sins, he is faithful and just and will forgive us our sins and purify us from all unrighteousness" (1 John 1:9). As we seek to live as God's light in our world, let us take our brokenness and sin to the Lord so that he can forgive us, heal us, and allow our light to shine brightly as an image of hope in a world that desperately needs one.

1. How does Psalm 38 describe the negative effects of sin on a person?

2. What specific insights into praying for forgiveness did you gain in your reading of Psalm 38?

3. Have you experienced the forgiveness of God in all areas of your own life?

THREE

Moving Past Despair

Psalm 39 *I said, "I will watch my ways and keep my tongue from sin; I will put a muzzle on my mouth while in the presence of the wicked." ²So I remained utterly silent, not even saying anything good. But my anguish increased; ³my heart grew hot within me. While I meditated, the fire burned; then I spoke with my tongue:*

⁴"Show me, Lord, my life's end and the number of my days; let me know how fleeting my life is. ⁵You have made my days a mere handbreadth; the span of my years is as nothing before you. Everyone is but a breath, even those who seem secure.

⁶"Surely everyone goes around like a mere phantom; in vain they rush about, heaping up wealth without knowing whose it will finally be.

⁷"But now, Lord, what do I look for? My hope is in you. ⁸Save me from all my transgressions; do not make me the scorn of fools. ⁹I was silent; I would not open my mouth, for you are the one who has done this. ¹⁰Remove your scourge from me; I am overcome by the blow of your hand. ¹¹When you rebuke and discipline anyone for their sin, you consume their wealth like a moth—surely everyone is but a breath.

*¹²"Hear my prayer, L*ORD*, listen to my cry for help; do not be deaf to my weeping. I dwell with you as a foreigner, a stranger, as all my ancestors were. ¹³Look away from me, that I may enjoy life again before I depart and am no more."*

Key Observation. When facing despair, God's people must put all of their hope in the Lord who invites his people to pray for his help and salvation.

Understanding the Word. Psalm 39 is a lament. If Psalm 38 serves as a prayer for forgiveness from sin, Psalm 39 deals with a time when the psalmist suffered in silence. There are times in our journey when we will fear sharing our pain or needs with those around us. Such times are profoundly lonely. The psalmist in Psalm 39 found himself in such a situation. His quiet suffering was magnified because enemies surrounded him. The psalm divides into four movements: verses 1–3, 4–6, 7–11, and 12–13.

Verses 1–3 establish the tone for the psalm. The psalmist took the stance of one in deep lament and desperate for God's help. The psalmist vowed to keep silent because he found himself in the presence of enemies. He did not want to share his thoughts or feelings out of a fear of his words being twisted for use against him. By refusing to speak, the psalmist also lost the opportunity to speak positive and good words. To remain silent in some situations is wise, but it is with our mouths that we make known the love and hope we find in the Lord.

The psalmist began his actual petition to the Lord in verses 4–6. But the psalmist's prayer followed a different path than what we've seen in the other laments thus far. The psalmist asked the Lord to show and remind him of the finiteness and irony of life. In the midst of his suffering, the psalmist was reflecting on the meaning and mystery of life. The psalmist recognized that life is short for both the good and the bad. Even those who gain wealth in this world cannot control who will ultimately spend it. In other words, as the psalmist despaired, he pondered the shortness of all life and his lack of control. How do we live when we feel as though our world is out of control and that we are spectators of our own lives?

In verses 7–11, the psalmist moved his focus beyond his despair to the one Being who stands outside of creation. He prayed to the Lord. How do we make it through this world? For the psalmist, there was only one way. He put all of his hope in the Lord who created the world and who invites his people to continue to pray for his help and salvation today. The psalmist was desperate to experience the cleansing of the Lord. We discover in these verses that the psalmist had been suffering due to his own sins and transgressions. He could not openly confess them because he feared the mocking and rejection of the wicked who surrounded him and would likely have not understood the inner struggle that was tormenting him.

In verses 12–13, the psalmist asked for the Lord's ear. He committed himself to the Lord and asked the Lord to take immediate action to bring relief to his suffering. He put himself in the posture of a marginalized person such as an immigrant in a strange land. Just as God had cared for his people when they were sojourners and strangers in Egypt, the psalmist anticipated God's kindness and grace to come through for him.

1. When does life seem the most out of control for you?

2. How does Psalm 39 teach us to pray when life doesn't make sense?

3. How do the words of Psalm 39 instruct you to respond to disappointment?

FOUR

Deep Trust in God

Psalm 40 *I waited patiently for the Lord; he inclined to me and heard my cry. ²He drew me up from the pit of destruction, out of the miry bog, and set my feet upon a rock, making my steps secure. ³He put a new song in my mouth, a song of praise to our God. Many will see and fear, and put their trust in the Lord.*

⁴Blessed is the man who makes the Lord his trust, who does not turn to the proud, to those who go astray after a lie! ⁵You have multiplied, O Lord my God, your wondrous deeds and your thoughts toward us; none can compare with you! I will proclaim and tell of them, yet they are more than can be told.

⁶In sacrifice and offering you have not delighted, but you have given me an open ear. Burnt offering and sin offering you have not required. ⁷Then I said, "Behold, I have come; in the scroll of the book it is written of me: ⁸I delight to do your will, O my God; your law is within my heart."

⁹I have told the glad news of deliverance in the great congregation; behold, I have not restrained my lips, as you know, O Lord. ¹⁰I have not hidden your deliverance within my heart; I have spoken of your faithfulness and your salvation; I have not concealed your steadfast love and your faithfulness from the great congregation.

¹¹As for you, O LORD, you will not restrain your mercy from me; your steadfast love and your faithfulness will ever preserve me! ¹²For evils have encompassed me beyond number; my iniquities have overtaken me, and I cannot see; they are more than the hairs of my head; my heart fails me.

¹³Be pleased, O LORD, to deliver me! O LORD, make haste to help me! ¹⁴Let those be put to shame and disappointed altogether who seek to snatch away my life; let those be turned back and brought to dishonor who delight in my hurt! ¹⁵Let those be appalled because of their shame who say to me, "Aha, Aha!"

¹⁶But may all who seek you rejoice and be glad in you; may those who love your salvation say continually, "Great is the LORD!" ¹⁷As for me, I am poor and needy, but the LORD takes thought for me. You are my help and my deliverer; do not delay, O my God!

Key Observation. Faithfulness flows from a dependence on the incomparable and great Lord.

Understanding the Word. Psalm 40 is an important psalm for reflecting on our walk of faith. It combines two distinct psalm types into one prayer. In verses 1–10, the psalmist gave thanks to the Lord for a past deliverance. In verses 11–17, the psalmist launched into a desperate prayer for rescue from enemies that he currently faced. The psalm teaches us to muster our past personal mountain-top experiences of God's grace as memories that sustain us when we reenter the valleys of life.

Psalm 40 opens with the psalmist recounting how the Lord faithfully delivered him from a serious challenge in the past (vv. 1–3). The psalmist faced death. This is the meaning of the reference to the "pit." It is a poetic way of describing the darkness of death. The psalmist's crisis moment had been averted by the saving power of the Lord. The psalmist cried out and waited; God delivered. The psalmist moved from a desperate pray-er to a delivered singer of God's praise. The psalmist had a "new" song. In other words, the psalmist became a testifier of God's saving ways to all who would listen. He saw his story as a means of connecting others to the same experience with the Lord.

At the heart of the psalmist's testimony was his steadfast trust in the Lord. Verse 4 deploys the word "blessed" (happy) that we've seen thus far in Psalms 1, 2, 32, and 146. It is the term that the Psalter uses to describe the happy state that God offers to his people. As we come to the end of Book 1, it is not a coincidence that the first two (Psalms 1–2) and the last two (Psalms 40–41) both use the word "blessed" (happy). Here in Psalm 40, *trust* is the key to a happy moment-by-moment existence. It is a trust that flows into a life of *faithfulness*. The psalmist described the life of faithfulness in verses 4b–10. It is a life of *dependence* on the incomparable and great Lord. There is no god like the Lord. The Scriptures tell the Lord's story and culminate in the victory that God works through the life, death, and resurrection of our Lord Jesus Christ. In response to the Lord's salvation and incomparability, the psalmist vowed to serve as God's ambassador through his life and words. He would live faithfully and passionately before the watching world as a means of pointing to his Savior. This is our call as persons who have received God's grace.

At verse 11, the psalm takes an abrupt turn. The psalmist suddenly moved from thanksgiving to desperation. Life works like this sometimes. Experiences of grace do not immunize us from challenges. What did the psalmist do? He had just sung God's praises for deliverance and now he was again facing extreme danger from enemies. Did he lose faith? Was he crushed? No. He immediately put his faith into action. He prayed fervently to the Lord for a renewal of mercy and saving love from this new challenge (vv. 11–13).

He asked God to deliver him from his enemies (vv. 14–15) and then ended the prayer with a word for the faithful and a confession of his own faith (vv. 16–17). He longed to continue to hear the faithful praising the Lord and serving as witnesses to the greatness of God. In other words, even in the midst of suffering, the psalmist remembered our mission as God's people. We live to serve as God's hands, feet, and mouthpieces to the world so that all may know of the Lord.

Last, the psalmist confessed his own need and his deep trust in the Lord. Given his past experience (vv. 1–10), he now waited for the Lord to act again.

1. What are some of the ways that you've encountered and experienced God's love and grace that serve as foundations for your walk with God?

2. In what ways does your past affect how you understand and endure suffering in the present?

3. What has your life taught you about trusting the Lord?

FIVE

Our Mission of Praise

Psalm 41 *Blessed are those who have regard for the weak; the* LORD *delivers them in times of trouble.* ²*The* LORD *protects and preserves them—they are counted among the blessed in the land—he does not give them over to the desire of their foes.* ³*The* LORD *sustains them on their sickbed and restores them from their bed of illness.*

⁴*I said, "Have mercy on me,* LORD*; heal me, for I have sinned against you."* ⁵*My enemies say of me in malice, "When will he die and his name perish?"* ⁶*When one of them comes to see me, he speaks falsely, while his heart gathers slander; then he goes out and spreads it around.*

⁷*All my enemies whisper together against me; they imagine the worst for me, saying,* ⁸*"A vile disease has afflicted him; he will never get up from the place where he lies."* ⁹*Even my close friend, someone I trusted, one who shared my bread, has turned against me.*

¹⁰*But may you have mercy on me,* LORD*; raise me up, that I may repay them.* ¹¹*I know that you are pleased with me, for my enemy does not triumph over me.* ¹²*Because of my integrity you uphold me and set me in your presence forever.*

¹³*Praise be to the* LORD*, the God of Israel, from everlasting to everlasting. Amen and Amen.*

Key Observation. We respond to God's grace with praise and faithfulness as we follow Jesus into the world on mission.

Understanding the Word. Psalm 41 begins in the same manner as Psalm 1. Psalm 41 is another psalm that points to the happy life. Psalms 1–2 both include statements about happiness so it is fitting that the final two psalms of Book 1 do as well (Psalm 40:4 and Psalm 41:1; cf. Psalm 1:1 and 2:12). Like Psalm 40, Psalm 41 mixes an assurance of deliverance with the ongoing need for the Lord's strength and help. It is part thanksgiving and part lament.

The psalmist opened with a saying about what constitutes a "blessed" (happy) life. It is a reminder that faithfulness includes caring for the poor and helpless in society. The life of faith is challenging. The laments testify to this, but God's people must continue to strive to live missionally relevant and focused lives. This involves loving God and loving neighbor. These themes come together when we practice justice and mercy for the poor. In verses 1–3, the psalmist reminded us that God sides with them and protects them from trouble and enemies. He brings healing to their lives. The psalmist believed this. It was the ground of his hope.

This becomes clear when the prayer shifts in verses 4–10 and we realize that the psalmist was asking for God's mercy. The psalmist's plea for mercy framed this section of the prayer (vv. 4, 10). The psalmist confessed his sins (v. 4) and put his future in the hands of the Lord. The psalmist suffered for two reasons: his enemies were gloating over his suffering, and he was struggling with an illness. His situation was compounded by betrayal at the hands of a close friend (v. 9). As we've seen throughout the Psalter thus far, the psalmist stood steadfast in the face of suffering and turned to the Lord for deliverance and mercy.

Verses 11–12 indicate that salvation arrived. Verses 4–10 become past tense and the psalmist reveled in his vindication by the Lord. Presumably this means that the Lord had healed the psalmist, but it also was clear that his accusers and afflicters had not prevailed over him. The psalmist testified of his close relationship with the Lord. He had lived faithfully. He walked with God daily. From the context of the psalm, it was vital to connect the psalmist's sense of personal integrity with the psalmist's faithfulness in caring for the lowly and despised of verses 1–3. This psalm indicates that he not only lived rightly but that he had experienced firsthand what it felt like to be among the poor and sick. The Lord has raised the psalmist up to be a healed helper of others and a proclaimer of God's mercy to the world.

This is a fitting conclusion to Book 1. The Lord calls us to live as his hands, feet, and mouthpieces in the world. The life of faith is not easy but the Lord is faithful to guide us on our journey and lead us into true happiness. Our response to this grace is praise and faithful obedience to the Lord as we follow Jesus into the world on mission.

Verse 13 serves as the concluding verse to the first forty-one psalms. It is a good word. It calls God's people to sing the Lord's praises for he is our God forever and ever. This is our security and hope. Amen and Amen.

1. How does Psalm 41 teach us to pray for mercy and justice?

2. How does Psalm 41 envision the happy life?

3. How did the psalmist model mission as a response to God's grace?

WEEK TWELVE

GATHERING DISCUSSION OUTLINE

A. Open session in prayer.

B. View video for this week's reading.

C. What general impressions and thoughts do you have after considering the video and reading the daily writings on these Scriptures? What specifically did this week's psalms teach you about faith, life, and prayer? What are some of the key impressions that our twelve weeks in the Psalms have left with you?

D. Discuss selected questions from the daily readings.

    1. **KEY OBSERVATION (PSALM 37):** We live faithfully by practicing goodness to others and placing our hope in God

    DISCUSSION QUESTION: What faithful practices can you embrace that may serve as a positive witness to the world about God's ways?

    2. **KEY OBSERVATION (PSALM 38):** God's people are able to bring their brokenness and sin to the Lord so that he can forgive, heal, and empower us to serve as witnesses to the world.

    DISCUSSION QUESTION: How does the psalmist teach us to pray when we've sinned?

    3. **KEY OBSERVATION (PSALM 39):** When facing despair, God's people must put all of their hope in the Lord who invites his people to pray for his help and salvation.

DISCUSSION QUESTION: When does life seem the most out of control for you? How does Psalm 39 teach us to pray when life doesn't make sense?

4. **KEY OBSERVATION (PSALM 40):** Faithfulness flows from a dependence on the incomparable and great Lord.

   DISCUSSION QUESTION: What are some of the ways that you've encountered and experienced God's love and grace that serve as foundations for your walk with God? What has your life taught you about trusting the Lord?

5. **KEY OBSERVATION (PSALM 41):** We respond to God's grace with praise and faithfulness as we follow Jesus into the world on mission.

   DISCUSSION QUESTION: How did the psalmist model mission as a response to God's grace?

E. Close session with prayer.